CHILDREN AND THE ARTS

CHILDREN AND THE ARTS

Edited by
David J. Hargreaves

Open University Press
Milton Keynes · Philadelphia

Open University Press
Open University Educational Enterprises Limited
12 Cofferidge Close
Stony Stratford
Milton Keynes MK11 1BY

and
1900 Frost Road, Suite 101
Bristol, PA 19007, USA

First Published 1989

British Library Cataloguing in Publication Data

Children and the arts.
  1. Schools. Curriculum Subjects. Arts.
  I. Hargreaves, David J, *1948–*
  700'.7'1

  ISBN 0–335–09881–9
  ISBN 0–335–09880–0 (pbk)

Library of Congress Cataloging-in-Publication Data

Children and the arts / edited by David J. Hargreaves.
    p.   cm.
  Includes indexes.
  ISBN 0–335–09881–9   ISBN 0–335–09880–0 (pbk.)
  1. Arts and children.   2. Arts—Study and teaching.
  3. Child psychology.   I. Hargreaves, David J. (David John),
1948–   .
NX180.C45C48 1989
700'.1'03—dc20   89–32656 CIP AC

Photoset and printed in Great Britain by
Redwood Burn Limited, Trowbridge, Wiltshire

Contents

List of contributors

Gavin Bolton: School of Education, University of Durham, Leazes Road, Durham DH1 1TA

Helen Cowie: Division of Education, University of Sheffield, Arts Tower (Floor 9), Sheffield S10 2TN

Maureen V. Cox: Department of Psychology, University of York, Heslington, York YO1 5DD

Lyle Davidson: Project Zero, Harvard University Graduate School of Education, Longfellow Hall, Appian Way, Cambridge, Massachusetts 02138, USA, and New England Conservatory of Music, 290 Huntington Avenue, Boston, Massachusetts 02115, USA

Maurice J. Galton: School of Education, University of Leicester, 21 University Road, Leicester LE1 7RF

Claire Golomb: Department of Psychology, University of Massachusetts-Boston, Harbor Campus, Boston, Massachusetts 02125, USA

David J. Hargreaves: Department of Psychology, University of Leicester, Leicester LE1 7RH

Susan Robinson: Department of Psychology, University of Leicester, Leicester LE1 7RH

Larry Scripp: Project Zero, Harvard University Graduate School of Education, Longfellow Hall, Appian Way, Cambridge, Massachusetts 02138, USA, and New England Conservatory of Music, 290 Huntington Avenue, Boston, Massachusetts 02115, USA

Dennie Palmer Wolf: Project Zero, Harvard University Graduate School of Education, Longfellow Hall, Appian Way, Cambridge, Massachusetts 02138, USA

Editor's introduction

David J. Hargreaves

This book aims to explain some of the processes which underlie children's artistic behaviour and development. Most of its authors attempt to do so from the point of view of developmental psychology, and the crucial question of the relationship between developmental psychology and arts education runs throughout the book. I shall argue that it is essential for these two disciplines to come together. On the one hand, developmental psychologists need to ground their research in the real world of children's arts – in the studio, classroom, rehearsal room or on the stage. On the other hand, arts educators urgently need a developmental basis for their discipline as well as some degree of rigour in their methodology and research.

There is widespread agreement amongst teachers, researchers and educators that it is vital to educate children in the arts: the arts provide unique opportunities for the development of personal qualities such as natural creative expression, social and moral values, and self-esteem. Paradoxically, there is also general agreement that this is not being done adequately: that the arts are grossly neglected in relation to other areas of the curriculum such as mathematics, reading or science. In the United States, a recent survey led to the conclusion that 'The arts are often considered to be frills, or even extra-curricular activities; and when the time for budget cutting is at hand, courses or teachers in the arts are likely to be among the first casualties' (Gardner and Grunbaum 1986: 1).

In Great Britain the same pattern of neglect was clearly apparent in the results of HM Inspectorate's curriculum surveys which were carried out a few years ago (DES 1982, 1983), as well as in a recent survey of initial training for primary teachers (Cleave and Sharp 1986). Similarly, the Calouste Gulbenkian Foundation's well-known national inquiry report *The Arts in Schools* (1982) argued that much higher priority should be given to arts subjects in the school timetable.

This issue has been thrown into sharp focus by the introduction of the

Education Reform Act 1988, whose statutes are being implemented in the British school system as this book goes to press. The Act is the culmination of a wide-ranging government review covering all aspects of curriculum content and assessment. The effects of the Act, which introduces a new national curriculum, are far-reaching, radical and controversial. Let me briefly mention three issues which impinge directly upon children and the arts; although these arise specifically from the new British legislation, the questions raised are of universal importance.

The first concerns the official status of arts subjects. The 'core' of the national curriculum is to consist of mathematics, English and science, to which first priority will be given. These will be complemented by the additional 'foundation' subjects of a modern foreign language, technology, history, geography, art, music and physical education. Now, whilst arts educators should presumably welcome the official recognition of art and music as 'foundations' of the curriculum, specialists in areas such as dance and drama are extremely gloomy about the prospects for their subjects: current indications are that these are likely to appear as appendages to subjects such as physical education and English rather than receiving proper recognition in their own right.

The second issue concerns changes in traditional 'academic' syllabus content in the arts: let us consider the specific case of music. *Music from 5 to 16* (DES 1985) is the discussion document prepared by HM Inspectorate which preceded the national curriculum plan for music. This document makes two fairly radical recommendations: that composition and improvization are to be included alongside re-creative performance and music literacy skills as integral parts of the curriculum; and that all forms of world music, including pop, folk, jazz and ethnic music, should be regarded as equally legitimate parts of the syllabus as Western 'serious' music. These changes will lead to a radical reappraisal of traditional practices for many British music teachers: and whilst they are probably more radical than those to be implemented in other arts subjects, the overall effect may nevertheless be a long-term reorientation of the status or 'legitimacy' of different art forms and idioms.

The third issue is that of assessment, which is especially difficult in the arts. One of the most controversial aspects of the new Act is the proposal that the educational progress of all children will be routinely assessed at regular age levels: 7, 11 and 14 years have been suggested as appropriate intervals. The extension of this to the arts subjects will present formidable problems, for a variety of reasons which are discussed in more detail in Chapter 8. The validity of conducting regular assessments presumably rests on the assumption that consistent age-related changes can be reliably observed in children's artistic development; but the contents of this book will show that this assumption is far from straightforward.

However, one way in which the new assessment procedures *are* in tune with current thinking in the research literature is in terms of teacher involvement. The new General Certificate of Secondary Education (GCSE) differs from the examinations it has replaced in that pupils are partly assessed by their own class teachers rather than by external examiners who have no knowledge of them other than a set of examination scripts. As we shall see, many psychological researchers are beginning to complement laboratory-based experimentation with naturalistic studies carried out in the real world of the classroom or playground. As far as assessment is concerned, the move away from standardized tests and towards the evaluation of specific course-work projects could be considered as a part of the same general trend.

The book is in three parts: Part I outlines the theoretical background. In Chapter 1, 'Developmental Psychology and the Arts', David Hargreaves sets the scene for the book by sketching a broad picture of the contributions which developmental psychology has made in this area. A discussion of some basic problems of definition is followed by reviews of the two major areas of research – the development of creative productivity, and theories of artistic development – and the chapter concludes with a look ahead at some directions for future research. In Chapter 2, 'Artistic Learning as Conversation', Dennie Palmer Wolf describes the way in which three *stances* develop towards artistic activity, namely those of the producer, the perceiver and the reflective inquirer. Focusing mainly (though not exclusively) on the visual arts, she argues that psychologists have neglected the mutual influences or *conversations* between these three stances and considers the implications of this reconceptualization for teaching and research.

Part II of the book deals with developments within artistic domains. In Chapter 3, 'Children's Drawings', Maureen Cox looks in detail at the strategies which children employ in the difficult task of making representations of three-dimensional objects on two-dimensional surfaces. Drawing on extensive evidence from her own research, Cox reaches the conclusion that tuition in basic drawing skills is more likely to liberate creative expression than to stifle it. In Chapter 4, 'Education and Development in Music from a Cognitive Perspective', Lyle Davidson and Larry Scripp undertake an ambitious synthesis of cognitive-developmental theory, issues in music education and research on musical development. Their cognitive-developmental model of music learning enables them to adopt a theory-based approach to some central pedagogical issues in music education, notably the use of computers in composition and the development of literacy skills.

In Chapter 5, 'Children as Writers', Helen Cowie considers the wide-ranging implications of viewing children as story writers. She describes how children create narrative sequences in play and drawings, and how this is related to the development of the concept of story. She also examines children's use of writing in the exploration of social roles and in the development of imagination, and discusses the part played by parents and teachers. In Chapter 6, 'Sculpture: The Development of Representational Concepts in a Three-Dimensional Medium', Claire Golomb draws attention to the scarcity of research on three-dimensional representation in contrast with the vast amount which has been done in two dimensions, that is primarily on drawings. The study of the former raises a whole series of theoretical issues which do not arise in the latter, and Golomb deals with some of these by describing her own well-known research on modelling the human figure. In Chapter 7, 'Drama', Gavin Bolton formulates an original developmental framework for children's drama. He describes the spectrum of dramatic behaviour in terms of the three modes of 'dramatic playing', 'illustrating' and 'performing a play', and spells out some of the implications of this framework for children learning to use drama form in educational settings.

Most of these authors are psychologists whose brief was primarily to write about developmental research in their specialist areas, bearing the educational implications of that research constantly in mind. Part III, on children and the arts in education, consists of a single chapter by David Hargreaves, Maurice Galton and Susan Robinson which looks specifically at the interface between developmental psychology and arts education. It is organized around three areas in which convergent developments seem to be taking place, namely psychological theories of learning and teaching; observational studies of classroom processes; and assessment in the arts.

I should like to express my thanks to Naomi Roth, Pat Lee and John Skelton for their help, encouragement and patience at different stages of the planning and preparation of the manuscript; to Howard Gardner for inspiration, encouragement and for putting me in touch with his Project Zero colleagues; to Elizabeth Eglinton for help with indexing; and, once again, to Linda Hargreaves for keeping me on the right lines in numerous ways.

References

Calouste Gulbenkian Foundation (1982). *The Arts in Schools: Principles, Practice and Provision*. London, Calouste Gulbenkian Foundation.

Cleave, S. and Sharp, C. (1986). *The Arts: A Preparation to Teach*. Slough, NFER.

DES (1982). *Education 5 to 9: An Illustrative Survey of 80 First Schools in England*. London, HMSO.

   (1983). *9–13 Middle Schools: An Illustrative Survey*. London, HMSO.

   (1985). *Music from 5 to 16*. London, HMSO.

Gardner, H. and Grunbaum, J. (1986). 'The assessment of artistic thinking: Comments on the national assessment of educational progress in the arts'. Unpublished paper, Harvard Project Zero.

Part I
Theoretical background

1
Developmental psychology and the arts

David J. Hargreaves

In this opening chapter I would like to set the stage for what is to follow: to delimit our area of enquiry and to outline the way in which the authors of this book go about it. Our concern is with children's activities of all kinds in what are conventionally called the arts subjects. Our primary aim is to delineate and evaluate the contribution of developmental psychology towards the understanding of these activities, and thus to the practice of arts education.

This would at first sight appear to be a reasonably clear-cut undertaking; but it certainly is not! There is a wide diversity of views about the appropriate usage of basic terms like 'children', 'the arts', 'aesthetic development' and 'creativity'. These are value-laden words which can have quite widespread connotations for different researchers and practitioners in the field. My aim in this chapter is to try to make some kind of sense out of the confusion of definitions, terms and understandings, and to outline the main theoretical problems which create it.

I should first like to establish my own working definitions of these central terms, which I hope should be acceptable to most developmental psychologists. This is followed by an account of the two major areas of general theory and research on children and the arts, namely studies of the development of creative productivity, most of which derive from the psychometric perspective, and theories of artistic development. The whole field is in an exciting stage of transition: we conclude with a summary of those issues around which the transition is occurring and with a prospective look at future developments.

Definitions and scope

'Children' and 'the arts'

Our interest is in trying to explain age-related changes in children's artistic behaviour, that is roughly between the ages of 1 and 11 years. But this raises a tricky question. Children are clearly different from adults in many important respects, but does it follow that the psychological processes underlying their artistic development are any different?

Until relatively recently, 'developmental psychology' was largely synonymous with the study of child development. The vast majority of empirical research studies investigated developments up to the age of 11 or so, and these were complemented by two much smaller, specialized areas of work on 'adolescence' (age range approximately 11–18 years) and 'ageing' (approximately 60 years plus). It is only in the last decade or so that developmental psychologists have come to realize that they have seriously neglected vast areas of their subject-matter. This belated realization has given rise to what has become known as the 'lifespan' perspective. Sugarman (1986) has formally set out the assumptions which underlie this, perhaps the most fundamental of which is that 'the potential for development extends throughout the lifespan. There is no assumption that the lifeline must reach a plateau and/or decline during adulthood and old age' (p. 2).

The result of this change is that there exists a 'tension between those who believe that the "interesting" aspects of development stop in adolescence (as did Piaget, for example), and those who believe that interesting development never stops' (Sternberg and Davidson 1986: 14). This raises a specific problem for the study of developmental processes in the arts. Some theorists would argue that there are certain ways of thinking about the arts which are unique to children, and in particular that stages of development can be specified in this respect. This line of argument originates from the theories of Piaget and finds its most elaborate and recent manifestation in the work of Parsons (1987), to which we shall return later in this chapter.

On the other side of the argument is the iconoclastic view of Howard Gardner (1973) that all the major developmental acquisitions that children need to equip them for fully-fledged participation in the arts, as creator, performer or audience member, have been made by the age of 7 or so. The implication of this is that the 'concrete operations' which Piaget specified as essential cognitive acquisitions in later childhood are not an essential part of artistic development. I am not sure whether it follows from this that Gardner could be described as a 'lifespan' theorist, and it is very likely that Parsons is just as interested in the developmental changes of adulthood as in stages in childhood. The implication is that although our primary interest is in children, we must be careful to spread the 'developmental' net as widely as possible.

The other half of my chapter title is equally tricky: what exactly do we mean by 'the arts' from the developmental point of view? Two main issues are raised by this apparently simple question. The first is whether individual art forms – literature, drama, dance, music, film and visual art – are quite separate and distinct domains or whether the processes underlying each are so similar that 'the arts' can be conceived as a unity. This is an important theoretical question for developmental psychology, and I will return to it later.

It is also a question which has generated extensive debate amongst arts educators. *Arts Initiatives I*, a report on the first congress of the UK National Association for Education in the Arts (NAEA 1986), for example, was devoted to a debate about whether or not the arts should be taught as an integrated subject. On the one hand, Abbs proposes that all of the individual art forms 'must be conceived as forming a single community in the curriculum ... they should be understood as serving similar aesthetic processes and purposes' (Abbs 1988: 3). On the other hand, Taylor, a music specialist, speaks of the 'evident problems and dangers of integrational, interdisciplinary or combined work' (Taylor 1986: 4), which include one art form subsuming another, or one art form being abused in the service of another. Taylor regards the differences between the arts as more fundamental than apparent similarities, such that the task of teachers should be to deepen understanding within each domain rather than to encourage superficial comparisons.

The second issue is just as difficult from the psychologist's point of view, namely that aesthetic and creative processes are by no means restricted to the arts subjects, whether these are regarded as unitary *or* domain-specific. The beauty of a mathematical equation or the elegance of a practical solution to a technical problem may produce a response in the trained observer which is just as worthy of description as an 'aesthetic experience' as is the art critic's response to a great painting. Major scientific discoveries like the double helix structure of DNA or Einstein's special theory of relativity are indeed commonly described in 'aesthetic' terms, and the work which led up to these discoveries is widely regarded as paradigmatic of creative thinking.

The popular and mistaken identification of the arts with creativity and science with problem-solving may partly arise from the way in which psychologists have gone about investigating these domains. There has been a distinct and regrettable tendency towards oversimplification: to analyse and attempt to measure complex phenomena in simple, numerical terms and to create conceptual dichotomies and statistical dimensions which do not necessarily have any basis in reality. The most obvious example of this is in the psychometric studies of creativity and intelligence, which represent by far the largest area of psychological research in this area. Psychometric researchers were able to distinguish empirically between divergent thinking, or ideational fluency, and convergent thinking, as measured by conventional IQ tests. But two misconceptions soon arose from this distinction. The first is that convergent thinking is equivalent to intelligence, as measured by IQ tests, and that divergent thinking is correspondingly equivalent to creativity. There can be little doubt that real-life creativity involves convergent *as well as* divergent thinking (and much more besides). As we shall see later, divergent tests have little predictive validity for real-life creative accomplishments. The second misconception is that scientific work tends to rely on convergent thinking,

and artistic work on divergent thinking. This is another massive oversimplification: creative (or even routine) work in both fields of endeavour involves
both types of process. If we link these two faulty assumptions together, we
emerge with the compound misconception that artists are creative, whereas
scientists solve problems.

There is a more deep-rooted aspect to this problem as far as theories of
child development are concerned. Piaget's theory, indisputably the most
influential single account, regards logical, scientific thinking as the ultimate
goal or 'end state' of development. One well-trodden line of criticism of the
theory is that this aspect of it leaves out many of the 'ludic' or 'antic' activities
which characterize the arts. Gardner, for example, writes that 'there is scant
consideration of the thought processes used by artists, writers, musicians,
athletes, equally little information about processes of intuition, creativity or
novel thinking' (Gardner 1979: 76). We seem to be left with a view of child
development which ought to be able to encompass the arts but which does not
as yet seem to have done so in any detail, and we are still faced with the
difficult question as to whether the essential features of artistic development
may also be present in children's scientific activities.

The moral of this initial survey of the scope of 'children and the arts' should
be clear. If we are to gain anything like a comprehensive understanding of this
multifaceted and under-researched domain, our study of 'children' must be
informed by a complementary view of the rest of the life span, and our
conception of 'the arts' must involve an implicit understanding of the complementary role of 'science'.

'Aesthetic' or 'artistic' development?

There is a great deal of confusion surrounding the use of these two adjectives.
My own innocent description of people's responses to a variety of musical
stimuli as 'aesthetic' led me into a great deal of heated debate in one conference presentation: this was primarily because my use of the term included the
everyday responses of non-expert listeners to popular music, rather than just
the high-level, sophisticated events which occur when the connoisseur hears a
great work. Similarly, a significant part of the debate which was sparked off
by *Aesthetic Development*, a discussion document produced by the Assessment of Performance Unit of the Department of Education and Science in the
UK (DES 1983), concerned the appropriateness of the title; indeed the
authors of the report concede, in their reflections on the comments received,
that 'Artistic Development' may have been a better title after all.

It would not be appropriate to pursue the philosophical issues in any detail
here; instead, simply and pragmatically, I shall propose 'working definitions'
of the terms which will at least enable us to proceed. The adjective 'aesthetic'
is the more general; it can refer to responses to all art forms as well as to
objects which are not conventional works of art but which are perceived in an
aesthetic context. Following Winner (1982), it seems reasonable to propose

that the context within which a symbol or object is perceived is an important determinant of whether or not it is perceived aesthetically. Thus a tree stump is not an aesthetic object to a farmer trying to clear his land of such obstacles, but it might well evoke a strong aesthetic response in a painter. Aesthetic responses are not only evoked by pleasing, beautiful or 'serious' art objects, of course; they can equally well be evoked by objects which are ugly, disturbing or mundane (and indeed some popular art forms, such as graffiti, deliberately exploit these features). Aesthetic development, correspondingly, can be regarded as the gradual acquisition of an increasingly sophisticated and differentiated repertoire of aesthetic responses.

Artistic development can be defined, more narrowly, as that which occurs in the behaviour and skills which are conventionally associated with arts subjects, as we described these earlier. In many cases there will be a close, overlapping relationship between aesthetic and artistic developments: the ability to create and perceive works of art will be based on the ability to appreciate natural phenomena aesthetically. But this may not always be true; artistic criteria may sometimes be of minor importance in aesthetic appreciation, and vice versa. As far as this book is concerned, this could be summarized by saying that most of the work to be described deals with artistic developments, as defined in terms of school subjects, and that these are likely to involve a substantial aesthetic component.

Creative production and aesthetic perception

Winner (1982) suggests that the four 'participants in the artistic process' are the artist, the performer, the perceiver and the critic – and that the psychology of art should deal with questions about all of these. The roles of the artist and the perceiver have so far received the most attention from researchers: 'A psychologist of art is interested primarily in the psychological processes that make possible the creation of and response to art' (Winner 1982: 8). Winner also points out that the perception of art has received more research attention than its production, probably because it is much easier to study in the laboratory and because it is a much more common part of the lives of most adults (unlike children!). Now this distinction poses another fundamental question for the student of children and the arts: can we propose generalized developmental processes which underlie creative production and aesthetic perception, or do we need separate theories of each?

There can be no doubt that the predominant theoretical influence in contemporary developmental psychology, and indeed in psychology as a whole, is that of the cognitive approach. The emphasis is on how people construct and manipulate mental representations of the world, and how these are manifested in intelligent behaviour. This approach is clearly and explicitly applicable to the arts, as can be seen from the title of a recent book edited by Crozier and Chapman, *Cognitive Processes in the Perception of Art* (1984). The editors provide an opening review of the major psychological theories of the arts, which they label 'psychoanalysis', 'Gestalt theory' and 'experimental psychology' (i.e. largely experimental aesthetics) and conclude that the study of cognitive processes can provide a framework for the integration of findings from these previously disparate perspectives.

In essence, the cognitive approach tries to explain behaviour by describing the structures according to which knowledge is organized and stored, and the processes which are carried out upon that knowledge, in between the input to the human cognitive system (usually an external stimulus) and the output from it (e.g. a behavioural response or a decision). Our question, formulated in these terms, is whether or not the cognitive processes underlying the development of artistic behaviour are the same for both production ('output') and for perception ('input').

This question may only ultimately be answerable within specific content areas, but there are already some clues which suggest that it does make sense to think in terms of general processes underlying production and perception. In the area of children's singing, for example, one of the leading researchers (Dowling 1984) speculates that it may eventually be possible to identify common 'schemata' (mental structures) underlying both music perception and production. A second clue is given by Serafine's notion of 'aesthetic creativity', which she defines as 'the process of being creative in that specific area defined as the sensory, aesthetic and artistic realm' (Serafine 1979: 257).

In the context of the American education system, Serafine sees this as representing the meeting-point between the 'creativity movement' on the one hand and the 'combined arts education and aesthetic education movement' on the other. Serafine's proposal is that the productive and receptive aspects of engagement with the arts are opposite sides of the same coin, and in particular that *aesthetic thought* acts in both realms. She gives a number of examples of particular activities with children which illustrate the point. In music, for example, children might listen to a piece and focus on loud/soft contrasts; this might then be linked to a group improvisation using sounds which explore the whole continuum from very soft to very loud sounds. The essence of the argument is *art as aesthetic understanding*, a long-standing principle in the world of art education (e.g. Abbs 1988).

So far, my speculations about the common ground between creative production and aesthetic perception have been at the most general level. Gardner (1973) provides an approach to the problem which is worked out in more detail and which forms an integral part of his theory of symbolic development. Gardner proposes that there exist three interacting 'systems' in development. The *making* system produces acts or actions, as seen in the creator or the performer; the *perceiving* system is concerned with discriminations and distinctions, which is the main province of the critic; and the *feeling* system deals with affect, which is seen in the audience member. The degree of interaction between these systems is held to gradually increase over the course of development, such that it eventually becomes impossible to separate any one of them from the effects of the other two.

Dennie Wolf adopts a very similar view, in Chapter 2 of this volume, in distinguishing between the three 'stances' which people can adopt in relation to art works, namely the producer, the perceiver and the reflective enquirer. Wolf sees these stances as 'multiple entry points into the aesthetic experience'. As with Gardner's three systems, she proposes that they frequently function together, in an integrated way. The degree of this integration, and its development with age, raises some difficult theoretical questions. Might it be, for example, that developments occur in children's aesthetic thinking which are so closely interrelated as to be independent of specific artistic media or can we only speak of 'stances' within a given domain? This is a central question to which I will return.

The development of creative productivity

J. P. Guilford gave his Presidential Address to the American Psychological Association on the subject of creativity in 1950, and this is widely regarded as a significant landmark: as the starting-point of the explosion of research on creativity which occurred in the next three decades and which still continues today. One of the primary reasons for this upsurge of interest was the educational climate of the time. There was a growing feeling that schools were defining giftedness primarily in terms of a narrow, restricted range of conventional school subjects, and in particular that the whole dimension of creativity, hitherto more or less ignored by teachers, should be given equal prominence in the curriculum.

This was accompanied in the psychometric research literature by a large number of investigations of the interrelationships between different measures of creativity, intelligence and school attainment. The pioneering study by Getzels and Jackson (1962) sought to establish that creativity, as measured by tests, was just as good a predictor of school attainment as conventional IQ; but numerous methodological flaws in the study meant that this conclusion was not in fact justifiable. Other researchers pursued the question in studies which overcame some of the technical problems (e.g. Wallach and Kogan 1965; Wallach and Wing 1969). Typically, different types of intelligence and creativity tests were administered to representative samples of schoolchildren under appropriate testing conditions. The aim was to show, by means of patterns of correlation, that these two dimensions were internally coherent; that they were largely unrelated to one another; and that they were equally good predictors of school success.

It may well be true that creativity and intelligence are of equal importance in school success, and indeed in later life accomplishments, but this kind of evidence hinges on the question of test validity. Children's performance on tests of creativity may tell us very little about their creative accomplishments in real life (see Feldman 1970), and the establishment of appropriate criteria of the latter is extremely difficult. For the moment, let us leave these problems aside and take the psychometric literature at face value. We want to know what this literature can tell us about the development of creativity in children. Perhaps surprisingly, only a few studies have addressed this question. The

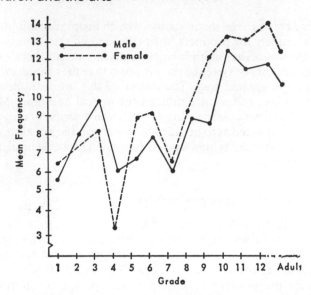

Figure 1.1 Developmental curve for the mean frequency of questions asked on the 'Ask-and-Guess' test.
(Reproduced from Torrance [1962] by permission of the author.)

most extensive research programme is that of Torrance (1962), and Arasteh and Arasteh (1976) have reviewed the whole literature.

Torrance has administered his own well-known 'Minnesota Tests of Creative Thinking' to large numbers of children from preschool age right through to graduate students, and so his results can be considered to be fairly robust. Figure 1.1 shows a developmental curve which he considers to be fairly typical: this shows the mean scores of males and females at one-year age intervals on the 'Ask-and-Guess' test. The test requires individuals first to ask questions about a series of pictures (prints from the *Mother Goose* stories, such as 'Tom, Tom the Piper's Son' and 'Little Boy Blue') which cannot be answered by looking at the pictures, and then to make guesses or formulate hypotheses about the possible causes of the events depicted, as well as to predict the consequences of them. The responses are scored for sensitivity to problems (number of information-seeking questions asked), ideational fluency (number of questions and guesses) and other measures of cognitive flexibility and originality.

Torrance considers that this curve describes some general features of children's creative development. There is a steady increase between the ages of 5 and 8 years, and then a sudden dip in the curve at the age of 9. This dip has been well-documented in other studies (e.g. Williams 1976; Hargreaves 1982) and has become popularly known as the 'fourth-grade slump'. The curve then recovers at the ages of 10 and 11 years, and another dip occurs at the age of 12, after which growth continues steadily until late adolescence. Torrance cites the work of researchers such as Andrews (1930) and Griffiths

(1945), which suggests that there may also be a dip in measures of creativity around the age of 5 years.

In summary, Torrance proposes that there are decrements in creativity test scores and in creative productivity at about ages 5, 9 and 12 and explains them in terms of transition points in children's educational careers. The first dip reflects the move from preschool into school: the 'fourth-grade slump' occurs as children move (at least in the American system) from primary into intermediate grades, and the dip at age 12 reflects the transition between elementary and high school. Torrance's argument is that these transitional periods are times of stress because children are adapting to new pressures and being forced to abandon their reliance on old attitudes and routines; the decrements in creativity performance are a direct result.

Torrance's account is very clearly rooted in the North American educational system; an acid test of the validity of his explanation would be provided by cross-cultural evidence collected from educational systems with different transition points. Unfortunately, systematic evidence of this kind simply does not as yet exist. My own investigation with British schoolchildren did in fact show something like a fourth-grade slump (Hargreaves 1982), even though the pressures of evaluation and assessment within the British system are probably much less intense. However, I would be extremely wary of imputing any kind of cross-cultural generality to this phenomenon.

I have only touched on the main features of the extensive psychometric literature on creative development in this section, but this at least conveys a feel for the basic approach, and for some of its limitations. Let me leave it by identifying three interrelated issues which make these limitations explicit and which thereby represent directions in which future research might profitably move. These are the measurement of products as distinct from people; the measurement of creativity within rather than across domains; and the identification of 'giftedness' in individuals.

First, one of the essential features of the psychometric approach is that it regards creativity (like intelligence) as a general, abstract characteristic of *people* which they possess in varying degrees. The premise is that a child's performance on a creativity test gives an indication of those mental capacities which are likely to predict real-life creativity. 'Creative potential' is seen as a kind of high-order, fluid skill, as yet uncrystallized around any given activity or domain. One problem with this, as we saw earlier, is that of test validity; the whole approach founders unless we can demonstrate that test performance shows positive correlations with indices of real-life creative productivity, and this also involves establishing what the appropriate criteria of real-life productivity actually are.

One way round the problem which was suggested long ago but which has only recently begun to gain currency, is to define creativity in terms of products rather than personal traits. Early work along these lines by McPherson (1963), for example, assessed the creativity of scientists in terms of the number of their patents, research reports, publications and so on. This work ran into difficulties because of the problems of establishing exactly how different products vary in their creative worth, and of dealing with products which remain unpublished, or fail to gain any formal recognition. Amabile proposes a 'consensual' definition of creativity which represents one solution to this problem; according to this, 'A product or response is creative to the extent that appropriate observers independently agree it is creative' (Amabile 1982: 1001). The assessment of creativity is accordingly carried out by independent experts who try to reach consensus about the relative creativity of a specified set of products within a given domain. Amabile (1983) has carried out an extensive series of assessments of students' artistic creativity using this technique. What this approach gains in ecological validity, however, it loses in generality; the assessments of creativity are restricted to the particular set of products under investigation.

This leads to our second general issue concerning psychometric studies of creativity: that their person-based orientation means that they are largely independent of specific domains of creative activity. Although there exist verbal creativity tests, graphic tests and even musical ones, the broad outcomes of the research which employs them are largely independent of the domain of creative expression. The putative developmental trends mentioned earlier, or the notion that creativity and intelligence (as measured by tests) are independent domains, for example, are seen as general propositions which are independent of the particular domain in which creativity might be manifested.

In particular, few distinctions have been drawn between the arts and the sciences in this respect, so we are led to presume that the development of the abilities underlying artistic creativity are the same as those for science, and presumably that these abilities are channelled into different directions according to the predilections and special interests of the individual. Whilst the question of the domain-specificity of creative development has received little attention within the psychometric literature, it has been a central issue in the study of aesthetic development. I will accordingly return to it in the next section.

The third issue involves the identification of particular individuals as 'gifted': can this be done across different domains of activity, and how is creativity involved? The psychometric approach leads us to believe that creativity, as measured by tests, is a normally distributed trait like IQ or height. Everyone is potentially creative to a greater or lesser extent, and the way in which this manifests itself depends on individual interests and special abilities. 'Creative' people, according to this view, are simply those who have more than the average of whatever creative potential is: they are quantitatively rather than qualitatively different from the majority of the population.

There is something rather appealing in this essentially egalitarian and 'demystified' view; it is supported by Weisberg (1986), for example, who refers to it as the 'incremental' view of creativity. It implies that the painting of a 7 year old may be just as creative within the context of that child's present activities as is a Picasso masterpiece to the art world, and that creativity can be observed in the mundane activities of us all. High levels of creativity arise from a combination of those essential abilities which are present in all of us, allied with specialized skills in a particular field and (just as important) high levels of motivation and hard work. It may even be that these 'secondary' factors are more important than high levels of creative potential: that there are no specialized psychological characteristics on which giftedness or genius depends. This contrasts with the more common 'mystical' view that creative people have special gifts which need special cultivation.

The whole question of giftedness, and its relationships with creativity and intelligence, has been the subject of a good deal of recent activity and debate (see e.g. Sternberg and Davidson 1986). There are essentially two opposing views of the origins of giftedness which have parallels with the two conceptions of creativity mentioned above. On the one hand, the existence of child prodigies and *idiots savants* in certain fields leads us towards some kind of biological explanation for precocity. On the other, the spectacular success of some preschoolers who have undergone extensive instrumental training under the Suzuki method, for example, shows that intensive environmental stimulation can also give rise to precocity. We emerge with a compromise: that giftedness requires both a predisposition towards exceptional skills in a particular field as well as the appropriate environmental conditions and stimulation. Gardner's (1982a) way of putting this is that certain individuals are 'at promise' for giftedness; that they will be able to attain exceedingly high levels of skill within a given domain given minimal exposure to the appropriate materials. However, they will not necessarily fulfil their promise; this requires not only the appropriate conditions and opportunities but also high levels of single-mindedness and motivation.

The psychometric research I have discussed in this section works on a fairly general level, and the three trends which I have identified all point the way towards specialization: the move is away from the universal and towards the particular. Let us turn next to those theories of aesthetic development which are specifically concerned with the domain of the arts.

Theories of artistic development

Psychologists have made various attempts to describe the course of artistic development within the specific domains which are covered in the chapters of this book. There has been relatively little effort devoted to the search for general explanations of these developments, though it seems fairly clear that cognitive models of development hold out the greatest potential in this respect. As in many other branches of child psychology, the starting-point for most models is the monumental, if nowadays somewhat controversial, theory of Jean Piaget. In this section I should like to contrast two prominent theories of artistic development. In spite of their differences, both of these are essentially cognitive explanations which have their origins in Piagetian theory. The first, proposed by Michael J. Parsons, is a direct descendant via Kohlberg: it is a cognitive-developmental stage theory which is explicitly based on Kohlberg's theory of moral development (see e.g. Kohlberg 1981). I have already touched on the second: Howard Gardner's theory diverges from the Piagetian model in several important respects – but I suspect that the differences may well turn out be in emphasis rather than in substance.

Parsons' (1987) book *How We Understand Art*, which turns out to be restricted to visual art, sets out his theory systematically. Parsons identifies three 'basic kinds of cognition' – the empirical, the moral and the aesthetic. The empirical deals with the external world of objects: the moral with the social world of norms, and the aesthetic with the inner world of the self. Parsons suggests that Piaget's theory deals most directly with the first of these; Kohlberg's theory with the second; and he sees his own theory as complementing the others within the aesthetic domain. The details of the theory are based on the results of large numbers of interviews (some 300 or more) which were conducted over the course of ten years or so with people ranging in age and experience from preschoolers to art professors. In each interview five or six paintings were discussed: the format was 'semi-structured' in respect of the pictures that were discussed, as well as of the questions asked. Numerous paintings and drawings were used over the course of the research, but eight of these were used repeatedly since they seemed to provide particularly rich and interesting data. These were *Guernica* and *Head of Weeping Woman with Hands*, by Picasso; Goya's *Lo Mismo*; Renoir's *Girl with a Dog*; Albright's *Into the World Came a Soul Named Ida*; Klee's *Head of a Man* (sometimes called *Senecio*); Chagall's *La Grande Cirque*; and Bellows' *Dempsey and Firpo*.

The questions asked in each of the interviews could be modified so as to follow up lines of argument which might be developed by individual subjects, but they were essentially based on a list of seven 'standard topic' questions, along with predetermined neutral 'probes' such as 'Can you give me an example?' and 'Whereabouts in the painting do you see that?' The seven standard topic questions were (1) 'Describe this painting to me', (2) 'What is it about? Is that a good subject for a painting?', (3) 'What feelings do you see in the painting?', (4) 'What about the colours? Are they good colours?', (5) 'What about the form (things that repeat)? What about texture?', (6) 'Was this a difficult painting to do? What would be difficult?', and (7) 'Is this a good painting? Why?'

Parsons' theory is directly modelled on that of Kohlberg in that he specifies cognitive-developmental *stages* as well as the salient *contents* of each stage. Parsons proposes five stages as compared with Kohlberg's six; although these follow one another in chronological order, he is wary of attaching precise ages to them. He specifies four broad areas of content, namely *subject-matter*, *expression*, *medium/form/style* and *judgement*. These become particularly important within stages 2, 3, 4 and 5 respectively, as we shall see next.

Stage 1 ('favouritism') is a precursor of these: its primary characteristics are 'an intuitive delight in most paintings, a strong attraction to color, and a freewheeling associative response to subject matter' (Parsons 1987: 22). The child's response to paintings exists primarily at an affective level, involving little cognitive discrimination – paintings are above all a means to enjoyment. In stage 2 ('beauty and realism') subject-matter becomes all-important. The child sees the primary purpose of the painting as being to represent something, and thus the degree of realism with which this is done is a primary factor in judging its quality. Parsons adds an aesthetic component to this in that children are also interested in the attractiveness of the picture. In summary, 'Beauty, realism, and skill are objective grounds for judgments' (p. 22). In stage 3, expressiveness becomes the salient characteristic by which pictures are judged: the emphasis is on the success with which the artist is able to express artistic intentions irrespective of the beauty or realism of the subject-matter. This represents a significant advance over the second stage in that it relies on an appreciation of the perspective of the artist.

In stage 4, form and style become paramount. Parsons sees this as an indication that paintings are social phenomena rather than individual ones: they are created and judged according to socially defined standards of taste and construction. Cultural traditions of artistic medium, form and style evolve over long periods of time, of course. They are matters of public debate, and new works of art are judged according to standards established as a result of previous works. The advance represented by this stage is therefore that the artist is able to judge his work in relation to the standards of the tradition as a whole.

Finally, in the fifth stage of 'autonomy', the artist realigns the relationship between personal and social standards of judgement so as to give prominence to the former – and this represents a change in emphasis from that of the previous stage. The artist is fully conversant with the social implications of working within a given style and can see his own efforts in that perspective, but he can also see at the same time that the work of individuals can lead to changes in the tradition – that standards are subject to negotiation. Many of the great artists have achieved their greatness by breaking rules rather than by following them, but this always occurs within the context of existing standards. In most cases, path-breaking artists display a mastery of the conventions of traditional styles before overturning them: Turner and Picasso are two obvious examples, and Debussy and Schoenberg provide musical parallels. The innovations of great creators such as these, after the initial shock has subsided, are almost invariably assimilated into the tradition.

Parsons has put forward an archetypal cognitive-structural theory which has a strong affinity with Piaget's original; as such, it is easy to level several well-trodden lines of criticism at it. I have discussed these at length elsewhere (Hargreaves 1986) and will not repeat them here. There are three other points, however, which apply specifically to Parsons' theory. The first, and most obvious, is that it is restricted to visual art, and this raises a number of issues concerning the extent to which aesthetic developments are domain-specific as distinct from general. Gardner has a good deal to say about this question, and so we shall defer its consideration until we have looked at Gardner's own theory. The second and third points concern the empirical evidence upon which Parsons bases his theory. The second is that all of the paintings used in this research are drawn from the 'serious' or 'fine art' tradition. We have no way of knowing whether the same theory would have arisen if commercial or popular art, for example, had been used as stimulus material. The third is that whilst semi-structured interviews have the advantage of flexibility towards individual subjects, they have the corresponding disadvantages of a lack of experimental rigour, and a reliance on subjective interpretation by the interviewer. We cannot be sure that Parsons' conclusions would emerge in the same way with a different subject sample or with different interviewers.

Having said this, it should be pointed out that comparable empirical work which has been carried out by other researchers does come to similar conclusions, and that a good deal of this work has been carried out on visual art (e.g. Machotka 1966; Gardner 1972). This brings us to Howard Gardner's theory, which is based on a large and impressive body of research carried out in a number of different artistic domains by members of the Project Zero group at Harvard University (see e.g. Gardner 1982b; Winner 1982). Although most of this research employs controlled experimental techniques, some of the group's work has used open-ended methods like those of Parsons. In one early study by Gardner, Winner and Kircher (1975), for example, children's conceptions of various artistic topics and media were investigated in a series of open-ended interviews with 121 4–16 year olds. Each child was shown a picture or read a poem or played some music, and asked a series of questions which covered seven pre-planned areas (the source, production, medium, style, formal properties and evaluation of art, and art's relation to the outside world). The interviews elaborated upon this basic outline by probing the children's thinking in each area along the lines of Piaget's 'clinical interrogation' techniques.

Analysis of transcriptions of the interviews led to the description of three levels of response to art, namely *immature* responses (concerned with the mechanisms and techniques of producing a work); *mature* responses, which revealed an understanding of the difficulties of producing art works, the differences in style between them and the properties of different artistic media; and *transitional* responses, which contained some features of each, as well as a prominent conception of art as striving towards realism. Although the details of this description are different from Parsons' scheme, it is easy to see that the two are broadly similar in orientation: both describe developmental changes in the cognitive structures underlying aesthetic judgement, which give rise to distinctively different types of response to art works at different age levels. Given this broad similarity, we need next to ask in what respects Gardner's view does differ from that of Parsons. Let me outline the main features of Gardner's theory before returning to this question.

I touched on two of its central aspects earlier in the chapter. First, I described his proposal that there are three interacting 'systems' in development (the making system, the perceiving system and the feeling system), the interaction between which is held to increase with age until they eventually become completely interdependent. This feature of the theory enables

Gardner to deal with the tricky distinction between effect and cognition in artistic behaviour; aesthetic objects simultaneously produce thoughts and feelings in the observer, and other theorists differ as to the relative prominence accorded to each of these. This feature also enables Gardner to deal with the problem of the distinction between aesthetic perception and creative production, as we saw earlier.

Second, Gardner's theory is primarily an account of the development of *symbol systems*. Symbol systems can either be primarily denotational (i.e. such that each symbol has a precise meaning, as in mathematics) or expressive (e.g. in abstract art, where symbols are not mapped precisely on to their referents). Gardner sees one of the primary tasks of developmental psychology as being to understand how adult competences in specific symbol systems gradually develop, and to explain these in relation to the development of cognition as a whole.

Two issues follow from this. The first, mentioned earlier, is Gardner's provocative view that all the major symbolic developments which are needed for fully-fledged participation in the arts have been accomplished by the age of 7 or so, so that there is no need for concrete operational structures of the type described by Piaget. The second is the view that developments in different symbol systems tend to occur independently of one another; that there is no need to postulate general cognitive operations which mediate age changes in artistic development as a whole.

These two issues seem to point up the main differences between Parsons, representing a straightforward cognitive-developmental approach, and Gardner. Whereas both try to specify the cognitive mechanisms underlying artistic development, Gardner (1973) rejects the idea of a series of general developmental stages which exist independently of individual symbol systems. He proposes instead that there are just two broad developmental periods, namely a 'presymbolic period' in the first year of life, during which the three systems unfold, and a 'period of symbol use' between the ages of 2 and 7 years. Gardner (1982b) discusses the differences between what he calls the 'specific-medium' and the 'general-symbolic' positions at some length, and begins by offering some powerful evidence in favour of the former from research in three different areas.

Claire Golomb's work on children's productions of human figures in specific media (drawing, clay and puzzle pieces) showed that the organization and articulation of these representations was strongly dependent on the nature of the task (Golomb 1974, and see Ch. 6 in this volume). Olson's (1970) research on the production and recognition of diagonals in different tasks (checkerboards, boards with electric bulbs, and toys) revealed that this ability was also strongly task-dependent, and Goodnow's (1971) investigations of children's representations of different sound sequences by drawing dots led her to the conclusion that specific 'tricks of the trade' were a more powerful determinant of performance on different tasks than were 'general skills'.

Further evidence for the same viewpoint comes from an ambitious study by

Winner, Rosenblatt, Windmueller, Davidson and Gardner (1986) in which the development of aesthetic sensitivity was measured on comparable tasks across three art forms. Winner *et al.* devised tasks of sensitivity to three aesthetic properties (repleteness, expression and composition) in each of three art forms (drawing, music and literature) and administered them to ninety children at each of three age levels (7, 9 and 12 years). There was a general improvement in performance on all the tasks between the ages of 7 and 9, and there was no evidence for any generalization of the ability to perceive the same aesthetic property across art forms, nor different properties within art forms. Winner *et al.* take this as strong and direct evidence for the 'medium-specific' position that aesthetic perception develops 'property by property, and domain by domain' (p. 149).

Although all of this evidence seems to provide strong support for the 'medium-specific' or 'multiple-media' view, Gardner (1982b) points out that its distinction from the general cognitive-developmental view may not be so clear-cut as is immediately apparent: we must be sure to take full account of children's differential training in and familiarity with specific artistic media. The 'medium-specific' position gives prominence to the specific skills and materials involved in different art forms whereas the cognitive-developmental or 'general-symbolic' view emphasizes the common properties of understandings in different art forms, thereby downplaying children's familiarity with specific media. In other words, Gardner tempers his predominantly 'medium-specific' view with the concession that there are also similarities in the ways in which symbolic developments occur across different artistic media.

He does this explicitly by proposing that children pass through a series of 'waves of symbolization' at approximately one-year intervals in early childhood. According to this proposal, there are four basic 'waves' whose effects can be identified across all symbol systems. 'Enactive representation' in infancy is the ability to organize actions into symbolic sequences. This is followed by the 'mapping wave', around the age of 3, in which relationships of space, size or distance can be captured in media such as singing or drawing. The third wave, 'digital mapping', involves a much greater degree of precision in representation, for example of pitch relationships in singing, or accuracy of detail in representational drawing. By the age of 5 or 6, the child becomes able to use cultural symbol systems such as musical notation or written language.

I have touched only very briefly on the notion of 'waves of symbolization'; the interested reader can find out more in Wolf and Gardner (1981) or in Chapter 2 of this volume. Its main interest to us here is that it represents a compromise between the two contrasting points of view. Gardner's main inclination is towards the view that the materials, skills, and symbol systems specific to each art form need to be studied in their own terms; but he simultaneously acknowledges that there are general age-related changes which occur across different domains. However, this by no means implies an acceptance of the existence of Piagetian-type stages, with all their connotations.

Prospect

The purpose of this first chapter was to set the stage for the rest of the book: to delimit our area of enquiry, to consider some problems of definition and conceptualization, and to outline the two main areas in which progress has been made. Let me conclude it by summarizing what we have learnt and by looking ahead. How might psychologists gain more understanding of children and the arts? The first point is that this topic must be studied in context. The study of children involves a complementary study of adults; the study of the arts involves an understanding of the development of scientific thinking; and the study of artistic production cannot be divorced from that of aesthetic perception.

The most obvious question for the developmental psychologist concerns age-related changes: can we detect any generalities in the development of children's artistic behaviour? This is a complex question to which a great deal of this chapter has been devoted. I think that the simple answer is yes – that there *are* distinctive age-related changes which can be observed in all children – but that explaining why and how these changes occur is extremely difficult. The best-known explanation is in terms of cognitive-developmental stages; this approach was initiated by Piaget, and its clearest present-day exposition is to be found in the theory of Michael Parsons.

Now whilst most psychologists would agree that age-related changes in artistic thinking can be identified, many would reject two central concepts of the Piagetian stage model. Some would reject the idea of developmental stages, which carry with them the implication of functional coherence amongst activities in different spheres. Second, some would not accept the assertion that generalized cognitive structures underlie developmental changes irrespective of the artistic medium and may prefer to speak in terms of age changes in specific processing strategies.

Putting these two views together, we might say that the current emphasis is on the identification of the mechanisms and strategies which underlie specific developments within given media or artistic domains. This emphasis is reflected in the rest of the book. The contributors to this volume all deal with the question of developmental change in relation to specific media, and to specific issues within those media. This is not to rule out the possibility of general similarities between developments in different media, such as Gardner's 'waves of symbolization', but the main emphasis is nevertheless on specifics.

This trend is accompanied by two complementary and interrelated movements. First, the investigation of general characteristics of people is increasingly being complemented by the study of specific products within a given frame of reference. This is particularly noticeable in research on the assessment of creativity. Second, many researchers are beginning to acknowledge the limitations of laboratory-based experimental techniques, and naturalistic investigations are coming into their own as a vital and indispensable part of their work. As we shall see in the final chapter, this trend goes well beyond the study of the arts: it has reverberations throughout the whole of developmental psychology. It holds out the promise of a much greater degree of reconciliation between psychological research and educational practice than has hitherto been possible.

References

Abbs, P. (ed.) (1988). *Living Powers: The Arts in Education*. London, Falmer Press.
Amabile, T. M. (1982). 'Social psychology of creativity: a consensual assessment technique'. *Journal of Personality and Social Psychology*, 43: 997–1013.
   (1983). *The Social Psychology of Creativity*. New York, Springer-Verlag.
Andrews, E. G. (1930). 'The development of imagination in the pre-school child'. *University of Iowa Studies in Character*, 3(4).
Arasteh, A. R. and Arasteh, J. D. (1976). *Creativity in Human Development: An Interpretive and Annotated Bibliography*. Cambridge, Mass., Schenkman.
Crozier, W. R. and Chapman, A. J. (eds.) (1984). *Cognitive Processes in the Perception of Art*. Amsterdam, Elsevier.
DES (1983). *Aesthetic Development*. Assessment of Performance Unit discussion document. London, APU.
Dowling, W. J. (1984). 'Development of musical schemata in children's spontaneous singing', in W. R. Crozier and A. J. Chapman (eds.), *Cognitive Processes in the Perception of Art*. Amsterdam, Elsevier.
Feldman, D. H. (1970). 'Faulty construction: a review of Wallach and Wing's *The Talented Student*'. *Contemporary Psychology*, 15: 3–4.
Gardner, H. (1972) 'The development of sensitivity to figural and stylistic aspects of paintings'. *British Journal of Psychology*, 63: 605–15.
   (1973). *The Arts and Human Development*. New York, John Wiley.
   (1979). 'Developmental psychology after Piaget: an approach in terms of symbolisation'. *Human Development*, 22: 73–88.
   (1982a). 'Giftedness: speculations from a biological perspective', in D. H. Feldman (ed.), *New Directions for Child Development: Developmental Approaches to Giftedness and Creativity*, No. 17. San Francisco, Jossey-Bass.
   (1982b). *Developmental Psychology*. 2nd edn. Boston, Little, Brown.
Gardner, H., Winner, E. and Kircher, M. (1975). 'Children's conceptions of the arts'. *Journal of Aesthetic Education*, 9: 60–77.
Getzels, J. W. and Jackson, P. W. (1962). *Creativity and Intelligence: Explorations with Gifted Students*. New York, John Wiley.
Golomb, C. (1974). *Young Children's Sculpture and Drawing: A Study in Representational Development*. Cambridge, Mass., Harvard University Press.
Goodnow, J. (1971). 'Auditory-visual matching: modality problem or translation problem?' *Child Development*, 42: 1187–201.
Griffiths, R. (1945). *A Study of Imagination in Early Childhood*. London, Kegan Paul Trench, Traubner & Co.
Guilford, J. P. (1950). 'Creativity'. *American Psychologist*, 5: 444–54.
Hargreaves, D. J. (1982). 'The development of ideational fluency: some normative data'. *British Journal of Educational Psychology*, 52: 109–12.
   (1986). *The Developmental Psychology of Music*. Cambridge, Cambridge University Press.

Kohlberg, L. (1981). *Essays on Moral Development*, Vols. I and II. San Francisco, Harper & Row.

Machotka, P. (1966). 'Aesthetic criteria in childhood: justifications of preference'. *Child Development*, 37: 877–85.

McPherson, J. H. (1963).'A proposal for establishing ultimate criteria for measuring creative output', in C. W. Taylor and F. Barron (eds.), *Scientific Creativity: Its Recognition and Development*. New York, John Wiley.

NAEA (1986). *Arts Initiatives I: Integration in the Arts*. London, NAEA.

Olson, D. (1970). *Cognitive Development*. New York, Academic Press.

Parsons, M. J. (1987). *How We Understand Art: A Cognitive-Developmental Account of Aesthetic Experience*. Cambridge, Cambridge University Press.

Serafine, M. L. (1979). 'Aesthetic creativity: thoughts on children's activities'. *Journal of Creative Behavior*, 13: 257–62.

Sternberg, R. J. and Davidson, J. E. (eds.) (1986). *Conceptions of Giftedness*. Cambridge, Cambridge University Press.

Sugarman, L. (1986). *Life-Span Development: Concepts, Theories and Interventions*. London, Methuen.

Taylor, D. (1986). 'Integration in the arts', in *Arts Initiatives I: Integration in the Arts*. London, NAEA.

Torrance, E. P. (1962). *Guiding Creative Talent*. Englewood Cliffs, NJ, Prentice-Hall.

Wallach, M. A. and Kogan, N. (1965). *Modes of Thinking in Young Children*. New York, John Wiley.

Wallach, M. A. and Wing, C. W. (1969). *The Talented Student: A Validation of the Creativity-Intelligence Distinction*. New York, Holt, Rinehart & Winston.

Weisberg, R. W. (1986). *Creativity: Genius and Other Myths*. New York, W. H. Freeman.

Williams, F. E. (1976). 'Rediscovering the fourth-grade slump in a study of children's self-concept'. *Journal of Creative Behavior*, 10: 15–28.

Winner, E. (1982). *Invented Worlds: The Psychology of the Arts*. Cambridge, Mass., Harvard University Press.

Winner, E., Rosenblatt, E., Windmueller, G., Davidson, L. and Gardner, H. (1986). 'Children's perception of "aesthetic" properties of the arts: domain-specific or pan-artistic?' *British Journal of Developmental Psychology*, 4: 149–60.

Wolf, D. P. and Gardner, H. (1981). 'On the structure of early symbolisation', in R. Schiefelbush and D. Bricker (eds.), *Early Language Intervention*. Baltimore, University Park Press.

2
Artistic learning as conversation*

Dennie Palmer Wolf

Introduction: art work as conversation

A 9 year old pores over a scrap of paper, marking, then humming to himself, then erasing and remarking. He is trying to notate a tune that he has composed with a small set of percussion instruments. He draws three bursts, 'See, here is where the music is supposed to go in three sharp bangs, maybe like car horns ...' (he plays these three elements for himself) ... 'no, like crashes' (he outlines these bursts again, heavily). Then he inscribes three upward arcs. 'Over here where the lines get longer, it's for the slower parts that come after.' (He stipples the paper with a zigzag of small dots.) 'Where all the dots are is for the part when you go up and down the scale' (he plays that portion from memory) '... Up, down, up.' He sits back and looks at his score. 'It's hard to get it right. I don't think I can write everything about it down.'

A 15 year old finds a reproduction of a Munch print in her portfolio of prints and begins to talk about why she saved it: '[When I look at Munch's print *The Kiss*] I notice right away how unevenly the figures divide the space. In my mind I imagine how different, how still, it would have been, if he had placed the figures dead centre. The figures have an extraordinary simplicity. Their features aren't defined. So in a way, more than the figures, you absorb the softness and roundness of the shapes. It's that that says, "This is a kiss."

'When I look at the one shape for two people, I think about the way he cut the block, getting those long lines ... hard as that is in wood. But I know that if I imagine the figures with elbows and lips, the power drains out.

'It is puzzling. Why do such simple shapes have that power? If I saw them anywhere else – in a magazine illustration, or in the middle of a print by Rembrandt – they would strike me as blobs.'

If these are the voices of young artists, then the sound of artistic process is decidedly polyphonic. Even though the 9-year-old musician has already

* The ideas on which this paper is based were first developed in a conference for arts educators sponsored by the Getty Center for Arts Education. The writing of this paper was supported with funds from the Rockefeller Foundation. I would like to thank numerous teachers in Boston and Pittsburgh for talking with me and allowing me to observe in their classes.

composed and played his tune, in order to notate it well (or well enough) he has to call on his experience as the composer ('What was I after here?'), his instrumentalist's perceptions ('How exactly did that go?') and his status as a reflective outside observer ('Can a notation really capture all?'). The same is true for the adolescent print-maker. At different moments she speaks with an empathy for the maker thinking about what it is to cut long, continuous shapes into the grain of wood and to dissolve figures into simple forms. At another moment she is out in front of the print, figuring out how its fused shapes say 'kiss'. In other moments she moves still further back, watching herself examine the print, sometimes groping for, sometimes fully sensing, how she reads this image differently from other prints or from other kinds of images.

If these are fair samples of developing artistry, then how children actually work at art or music or writing and how we study that activity have traditionally been mismatched. Studies of growth or learning in the arts have long been striated; for example, in the visual arts there are studies of children's drawing development, studies of picture perception and studies of children's understanding of visual art. Rarely, if ever, have there been observations or experiments that look either at all these abilities in the same children or, more importantly, at the conversations or mutual influences among these abilities. There are probably significant costs to that mismatch. First, there is the cost to accurate description: we risk mistaking traditions within the adult practice of the psychology of art for the natural kinds in children's artistic activity. Second, and perhaps more significant, if drawing, seeing and thinking (or composing, playing and reflecting) really do 'speak' to one another, in treating them separately, we risk ignoring a major source of change or development in artistic learning. It is at least possible that the young musician who realizes the limits of notation comes to think more deeply about an instrumentalist's right and obligation to interpret, rather than just to play, a score. Plausibly, an adolescent print-maker who has thought about the fused shapes in Munch goes to her own next work with different questions about outlines and contours.

In the spirit of investigating these possibilities, this chapter presents a sample of how we might reconceptualize aesthetic development based on the notion of shifts in the conversation between several continually developing stances toward artistic activity: that of the producer, the perceiver and the reflective enquirer. The particular form of artistic activity sampled is the visual arts – simply because it is in that domain that we have the greatest numbers of studies and observations. (However, examples from other domains have been included in order to suggest how widely applicable this reconceptualization might be.) Exploring such a reconceptualization is complex and requires several steps. The chapter begins by outlining some underlying assumptions. In a second section three periods of growth in the visual arts are examined: the advent of picture-making (3–6 years), the understanding of visual systems (7–12 years) and the grasp of renditions (13–18 years). Each of them is described as the result of interactions among children's productive, perceptual and reflective capacities. Finally, in closing, questions are raised concerning what such a reconceptualization means for teaching and research.

Beginning assumptions

The comparative psychologist Heinz Werner was fond of pointing out that without a teleology – without specifying a goal towards which growth moves – it is impossible to distinguish raw change from development. Freud argued that human development moves toward the eventual regulation or civilization of basic drives, while Piaget saw logical thought at the end of the tunnel. By contrast, thinkers in the tradition of Kant or Habermas would argue that there is not one but rather multiple end-points to development: a varied affective and moral life, the generative exercise of thought and the creation (or re-creation in perception) of aesthetic experience (Parsons 1987). Taking this point about variety a step further, it is possible that our teleologies, even within these domains, have been far too monolithic. Within affect, morality or aesthetic learning there may be multiple lines of development – a diverse family of understandings or processes which may mature or progress at varying rates and towards distinctive ends. In the realm of the aesthetic, we see a set of potentially separate processes at work in the earlier example where a young artist uses several bodies of knowledge, or stances, in order to arrive at what Munch's print means. At one moment she draws on her knowledge as a maker, later she acts largely as a perceiver, during a third moment she stands back, reflecting her own aesthetic thinking.

It is important to define these three stances more closely:

1. The producer: In this stance, an individual is 'in the middle' of the work, engaged in questions like 'How is it possible that pigments and lines could map out the fat lobes of a ripe peach or the exact way the down mutes its yellow skin?'; 'What happens if I cut this image as a wood block or make it an etching?'; or 'How can a painted room convey a sense of order or doom?'
2. The perceiver: From this stance an individual stands outside a work, looking on. A perceiver concentrates on noticing and comparing, asking 'What is this I see?'; 'In how many ways is this image meaning?'; 'What here calls to mind other images?'; 'How do those evoked images inform my understanding of what I behold?'
3. The reflective enquirer: From this stance an individual stands far back from a work (his own or someone else's) and poses questions like 'How is this image different from a sign or a dictionary illustration?'; 'Why is it hung on the white walls of what looks like a bank or a treasure house?'; 'How does that control the way I, and others, see it?'

It is tempting to describe these stances in terms of recognizable cultural end-points, arguing that the stance of producer has at its centre the kinds of abilities and insights common to studio artists or that the stance of a perceiver is closely akin to the work of an art critic or historian. But if we look closely at moments of naturally occurring aesthetic experience, in artists, critics, historians or even less-specialized viewers, we find that all these individuals spontaneously move among the several stances – as a way of taking different perspectives on or having a conversation about a work. The stances offer multiple entry-points into aesthetic experience. When they function together, in an integrated way, they greatly expand visual experience. They are, when well taught and fully exercised, like Braque's Cubist images of tables or violins: versions which enhance and confirm the integrity and the multiplicity of visual experience.

The development of several stances: understanding pictures, systems and renditions

In the following section I suggest that we can, on the basis of developmental and educational research, discern at least three very broad phases in the development of aesthetic knowledge. Each of these phases is the result of what I would call *dialogues* between what children can produce, perceive and reflect on. In working out this sequence, I have used developmental research pertaining chiefly to visual experience. I have not, for instance, appealed to Piaget as suggesting the limits for what can and cannot be understood in a painting. This is out of a conviction that human knowledge is more specialized than it is general and that the kinds of principles that govern logical thinking may offer some, but hardly a full, explanation for why aesthetic skills develop as they do. We would, I think, lose much of what is specific, even unique, to aesthetic knowledge, if we were to submerge it with other forms of knowing (Gardner 1983; Parsons 1987).

From 2 to 6: the understanding of pictorial symbols

In infancy children build up a storehouse of sensations, routines and expectations. From this experience, they make practical sense out of their physical and social worlds. Based on this experience, between 2 and 6, normal children take the tremendous leap from being exploratory animals to becoming symbol-using human beings. They acquire the fundamental grammar of their native language (Brown 1973), the rudiments of a number system, and the conventions that govern the music they hear and sing (Davidson 1983). One consequence of this burst of symbolic development is that children who have only been picture-readers (Deloache, Strauss and Maynard 1979; Hochberg and Brooks 1962; Jahoda, Deregowski, Ampene and Williams 1977) join the community of picture-makers (Golomb 1974; Kellogg 1969; Smith 1972, 1982; Wolf and Gardner 1980). This means, quite simply, that they begin to understand the demands and power of graphic representation. In fact, even 3 year olds make a reliable distinction between what they call 'pictures' and 'designs' – marks which symbolize and those that simply create patterns.

But young children realize that marks do more than refer: they can also transform or create information. A 3 year old can read a wobbly circle enclosed by a large oval as 'a ghost with a stomach'. A 4 year old can draw a completely fantasy event: the imagined meeting of two American super-heroes, Superman and Big Bird. Moreover, between 3 and 5, children also grasp the peculiar demands of visual symbolization. At 3, a child drawing Mickey Mouse makes his belt by drawing a line which literally encircles the paper front to back. However, at 5 he understands that in a picture he can draw only what shows in the picture plane (Wolf 1988a) and depicts only that portion of the belt which would be seen from the front.

There is considerable research which portrays very young viewers as looking through, rather than at, visual displays. They rarely notice style, composition or the multiple meanings in pictures made by others (Machotka 1966; Parsons 1987; Parsons, Johnston and Durham 1978; Walk 1967; Winner 1982). Children at these ages make few distinctions between images and the world of objects pictures represent: young children gravitate to pictures of things they like and reject as ugly pictures of violence, frightening items or objects they personally dislike (Parsons, Johnston and Durham 1978). Consequently the criteria for aesthetic judgement appear to be simple: 'If I like what it pictures, it's good.' Similarly, children this young make little distinction between what they like and what others might like. What may be key here is that young children can attend to only one aspect of a picture at a time. For example, under the age of 7, if shown a figure made with an apple for a head and bananas for legs, young children cannot see the contours as part of both the man and the fruit (Elkind 1970). But without this kind of double vision it is hard to see aesthetically as there is no way to understand how the qualities of the forms underscore or undercut their meanings.

However, this harsh view of young children's perceptions may be the result, at least in part, of the particular formalist sensibilities central to Western and modern art scholarship. As expressionist and narrative currents become stronger in our thinking about art, we begin to have a clearer sense of what is promising and generative in the way that young children apprehend and respond to visual images. For example, when children use what may be their richest form of knowledge – their feel for situation, characters, narrative and scene (Nelson 1986) – they can draw detailed inferences about the world pictured. Thus, in looking at Seurat's *La Grande Jatte* a 6 year old can imagine her way into that world:

> If I was in that park, it would be noisy. The people would be talking. Maybe one of the mothers is yelling to a kid not to go too close to the water. And the dog might bark at the monkey. And there's wind blowing for the boats.

While she fails to notice (or talk about) styles or symbols, this child understands that the painting is 'a world' with its own rules which are not necessarily those that bind the men, women and children she encounters in her everyday life. Asked to imagine what else Seurat might have chosen to paint into his park if he had had two more feet of canvas off to right, she continues:

> C: Maybe . . . I think he would have put some more trees like these with the white trunks and the little leaves. And a family coming to have a picnic on the river. Two kids . . . a girl in a blue dress and a boy running after her and then the mother and father with a big basket.
>
> I: What would the father look like?
>
> C: (pointing to one of the frock-coated gentlemen): Like this one, with a straight-up hat and one of these coats.

Not only does she expect that the trees in the new section of the painting will be the birches of the Paris summer, but that the father in this world will have the look of a frock-coated gentleman rather than the casual appearance of her own father. Typically, we think of being able to read a painting in much more purely visual and formal terms. But this child's responses remind us that part of understanding and interpreting a work like *La Grande Jatte* involves being drawn deeply into a particular time, space and light.

Nor is this kind of narrative inference the only way in which young children can read more than pictorial reference. Research on early metaphor suggests that as early as their third year children view and describe their visual experience in figurative ways (Winner, McCarthy, Kleinman and Gardner 1979). Staring at the tangle of lines left by scrubbing at a paper with a bright blue marker, a 3 year old calls out, 'Big blue fires burning.' With this, she links the intensity of her own motions with the way the lines lick out across the white paper and that fires burn. This is what Werner and Kaplan (1967) call physiognomic perception – a mode of experience common to children in which the links between the several senses, affect, and bodily response become sharply prominent. This ability to defeat the usual categories of apprehension is not merely charming or childlike. Think how much the reading of a Rothko painting depends upon being able to see the sombre fields of colour as trembling, descending or soaring.

We know perhaps the least about young children's capacities to take on the role of the reflective enquirer, someone who thinks about how she or he (or someone else) thinks about pictures. Moreover, what we do know presents a curiously chequered portrait. On the one hand, research by investigators like Tizard and Hughes (1984) shows that children as young as 4 can pursue long arcs of questions about visual phenomena that puzzle them (such as why you only see half a cow at the edge of a book illustration). But other recent work indicates how these enquiries take place within important limits. To begin, young children have difficulty second-guessing or examining their own most immediate perceptions. In interviewing young children about the differences between appearance and reality, Flavell, Green and Flavell (1986) found that children struggle with the idea that the colour red lent by a piece of cellophane does not inhere in the object covered by that cellophane. Similarly, the way young children understand the workings and products of the mind is still incomplete (Wellman 1987): they have difficulty understanding how a person might say or show one thing and mean either several things or something quite different. Thus, at the moment when they have a grasp of the image-making process, young children lack the skills to 'second guess' that image. They cannot imagine it other than it is – hence, they cannot imagine how it might function as one choice among numerous alternatives. Altogether, the absence of this hypothetical frame suggests why young children's enquiries about paintings and drawings are often limited to the images as they are rather than how they might be.

A second point is that young children lack well-defined concepts of different types of visual activity; for instance, they make few distinctions between (potentially) aesthetic and non-aesthetic objects, such as maps and drawings (Liben and Downs 1987). Even when they recognize a map, they will still argue that the upper portions in a map represent the sky, while the lower regions show where the buildings and ground are. Hence, young children's thinking about drawings and paintings may be limited because they do not yet think in terms of special classes of visual images or experiences each distinguished by particular qualities. While young children understand a great deal about the power of visual images, for them a billboard, a book illustration and a painting all work in the same way. Until young children come to think about the individual mind behind the work and the cultural activities within which an image takes on meaning, children's perceptions and reflections about pictures remain germane to the realm of visual experience, but fundamentally not to the aesthetic.

Even as preschoolers, young children can take at least two stances on their art work: that of a producer and a perceiver. The second and less familiar point is that artistic development may actually occur because of children's ability to juggle their activities as artists and viewers. For instance, children's earliest representational drawings often emerge as a result of a dialogue between production and perception. The following observation of a 3 year old who had never drawn representationally is suggestive:

> J sat drawing a series of wavering closed forms. On one try he inscribed an upright triangular shape, probably quite by accident. He sat back, turned the paper so that the point was upwards and pronounced it 'boat'. Based on that reading, he went back to drawing. First he added a series of short, wavy lines under the triangle, calling out 'water'. Subsequently, he added two dots inside the triangle, calling them 'people'.

J's drawing emerges from the back and forth between what he makes and what he sees in what he makes. It is his knowledge as a viewer that leverages and challenges his abilities as a picture-maker.

From 7 to 12: the understanding of visual systems

Children's uniform approach to visual images begins to break apart as they become acquainted with the particular range of visual languages or systems which their culture distinguishes. Across cultures, by the age of 7, children begin formal training in adult-like tasks of their particular culture – whether that is herding, hunting or reading and writing (Whiting and Edwards 1973; White 1970). In any culture this is the period in which we require children to adopt explicit versions of the thinking skills and codes they will need to survive in their particular society: the formal codes of counting, reading and writing, as well as the major categories for understanding human action: right and wrong, play and work, possibly even mundane and aesthetic (Erikson 1963). It has often been argued that this welter of rules contributes to what is often called a literal, or highly conventional, phase in children's productive development (Winner 1982) where drawings are formulaic and clichéd. However, when closely examined, this is not necessarily a 'flat' or uncomplicated period in aesthetic development.

It is not surprising that in this context of learning the basic categories of human life and activity, children's understanding of visual images grows more systematic. As makers, children become absorbed with learning the 'tricks of the trade' that make things 'right' – how to draw Charlie Brown or make a deceptively three-dimensional cube out of just lines. In this way, school-age children avidly acquire symbolic recipes – the conventions of popular illustration (e.g. thought bubbles, zoom lines, tricks for making noses and muscles) (Gardner 1973; Lowenfeld 1957; Willats 1977; Wilson 1974; Wilson and Wilson 1977) or the studio demands of careful observational drawing (Smith 1987). Such attention means that children become keenly aware of the different systems, or genres, of image-making that flourish in their culture. For example, they begin to distinguish between maps and drawings (Liben and Downs 1987) or between different types of drawings. When 10 to 12 year olds are asked to finish drawings with and without aesthetic properties like expression, they accurately match their own drawing styles to that of the original drawing (Carothers and Gardner 1979). Similarly, when asked to make birds that would appear in a science report, a zoo sign and an art gallery, pre-adolescents produce distinct forms. For the report, a child might draw a blue jay in careful but not interpretative detail; the zoo sign is a spare, generic contour drawing; the art gallery bird is richly coloured and fantastically detailed (Wolf 1984).

This sense for the system of choices behind an image informs the relations *within* children's works as well. For the first time children make what appear to be conscious choices, not just about content or genre but about stylization in their own works. For instance, in painting night in the city a 10 year old might portray just the dark towering forms of the skyscrapers with their lines of yellow lights, deliberately leaving out traffic, street lamps and pedestrians. Moreover, the young painter begins to think about his work as a network of related choices: if he paints the buildings loosely, with long strokes of sombre blacks and greys, the sky behind them is likely to have something of that feel (Smith 1982). In so doing, pre-adolescents become alert to the choices, not just the depictive obligations, of rendering visual experiences.

This awareness of the systematic nature of visual images has interesting ramifications for the ways in which pre-adolescents take on the stance of both observers and reflective enquirers. On the one hand, their keen awareness of rules means that they are often troubled by, or intolerant of, works in which the expected rules are broken, finding them puzzling, weird or ugly (Parsons 1987). They have fixed expectations: just as all poems should rhyme, all paintings should be recognizable pictures of handsome, valuable or interesting items. In other words, the same things that make a machine, building or tool seem impressive are valued in paintings or poems: size, complexity, a high price tag, power, strength (Child and Iwao 1977; Machotka 1966; Parsons, Johnston and Durham 1978). Limiting as the point of view may seem, implicit in it is the ability to pay attention to the material presence of a work. For example, when asked what his favourite object was in an exhibition of Chinese artifacts, one 8 year old replied:

> I liked the jade sword that was right by the door. It was longer than 6 feet. The guy who used it had to be real strong. I think they used it to chop off people's heads. Because Dan and I looked at it up real close and we could see some rusty brown stuff that maybe was old blood.

Pre-adolescents' sensitivity to system and to the material qualities of works can, if tapped in thoughtful ways, be used to alert them to the particular ways in which aesthetic images work. In particular, they can extend their earlier understanding of depictions (pictures) to quite a range of drawing systems, including the styles of individual artists. For example, with teaching, children can learn to see 'through' an image, looking instead for the style or mood of a work (Deporter and Kavanaugh 1978; Gardner 1970, 1973; Walk 1967). For the first time as viewers, children can begin to recognize that images function in a number of ways. Van Gogh's chair both denotes 'a chair' and shows one – out of several possible – ways of drawing it (Elkind 1970; Silverman, Winner, Rosenstiel and Gardner 1975). With the advent of this kind of visual thinking, school-age children – if encouraged – can begin to understand how a visual image is both referent and form.

Still other veins of research suggest that between 7 and 12 children think much more flexibly and reflectively about their experience. Work concerning their conceptions of mind suggest that after 7, they can think about the motives which underlie behaviour (Wellman 1987). Quite possibly this opens up to them questions of what an artist might have been trying to effect in a viewer. Pre-adolescents can look at a Paul Strand photograph and ask why the photographer might have chosen to picture a machine at such close range and what the effect might have been if he had shot it at an enormous distance. As their hold on the reality–appearance distinction firms, they can think about things other than as they literally are (Flavell, Green and Flavell 1986). This means they can look at a painting or drawing and consider how else the work might have been made. They can be engaged in looking at *The Bathers* by Picasso and talk about how it is different from a National Geographic photograph of swimmers on the beach at Cannes.

During their school years, children's capacity for reflection and criticism grows. As they become aware of the rules that govern different types of visual images, they also become acutely attuned to what constitutes deviance from those rules. Growing up in a culture that values illusionistic drawing, school-age children are strongly critical of their own and others' drawings whenever those images break step with realistic rendering (Rosenstiel, Morison, Silverman and Gardner 1978). Thus, while younger children tend to use their production and perception capacities heavily, school-age children's thinking about the visual arts is informed, and in some ways sobered, by the emergence of their own critical and reflective capacities. What emerges is a complicated three-way approach to visual work, in which making, looking and appraisal all contend. This sample of a 9 year old drawing is illustrative:

> K is making a marker drawing of a scene of grass and trees. She draws two girls facing each other and a ball high in the air between them. She pauses, looking somewhat frustrated. 'It looks like a dish.' She calls out to her mother who is in the kitchen, 'How do you make a ball look round?' Her mother calls back, 'Draw it round.' K says, 'No, fat ... all around.' There is no answer from the kitchen. K takes out the orange marker and tries drawing what looks like a halo around the ball. She sits back on her haunches and stares at the image. She goes to a bookshelf where she looks up a playground scene in a Richard Scarry book. She tries copying the motion lines she sees there on her own drawing, but doesn't like the effect. She takes out the red marker and really scrubs the colour down. Disappointed, she carries the drawing into the kitchen explaining, 'All I can think of is to draw it on the back, but that's not how drawings go.'

Like the young musician observed at the start of this paper, K makes use of all three stances in making her drawing. It is the interaction among these stances which allows her to realize and pursue the differences between drawing a round (having a circular contour) and a fat (being spherical) object. As a producer, she experiments with different approaches to make a three-dimensional object appear on a two-dimensional surface. But those experiments are guided by what she can perceive about the effectiveness of her own work and the conventions used by other artist-illustrators. Reflecting on her drawing problem, she comes to her conclusions about the limits of her system of drawing.

From 13 to 18: the understanding of rendition

Adolescence brings two major changes to the apparently systematic world of the school-age child. Each of these changes has to do with understanding choice. Perhaps the most famous of these changes is the turbulence associated with body changes, independence and a search for personal identity (Csikszentmihalyi and Larson 1984; Erikson 1968). The second, quieter but just as profound shift derives from the adolescent's ability to think about alternatives to 'what is'. Put differently, adolescents are capable of entertaining for themselves and recognizing in other people the making of choices. In the world of visual experience, we can think of this as understanding and appreciating the options of rendition – not just whether you want to make a map or a drawing of a landscape, but what it is you want to say about the way the fog . riddles the landscape and just how you will make the smoky lines coming out of the end of the graphite pencil 'say' these things.

This interest in selecting a powerful means to convey an experience or an ideal is evident when this adolescent artist remembers making a series of sea-shell drawings:

> Last term I started drawing sea shells. I wanted to learn how to draw things from life, so I decided to draw the same object over and over and over. While I was working on them, I started to see a lot about different kinds of lines. Shells force that – as you move around drawing one of them, you have sharp edges, folds, flaps, round shoulders. I went from pencil to charcoal because I couldn't get the pencil to do all that. But with the charcoal you can get a hard edge and blurry soft forms. The more I worked, the more I saw each one of the lines as a 'story'. It would start at the front edge all clear and hard and then travel up towards one of the shoulders and I would have to change it, make it thicker and softer, as it went.

In fact, the very making of a series of drawings – something one begins to see in high school portfolios – implies more than common teaching practices. It is an indication that high school students are very much concerned with the issue of rendition, that is, how to understand what it is to generate any number of versions and to select the most successful or powerful instance.

Adolescents are also interested in considering what kind of message they want for a work. Whereas younger children focus on picturing families, buildings and animals, adolescents begin to use those familiar forms not merely to denote but to symbolize and communicate messages about peace, freedom and self. This understanding that works can send complex messages or evoke impressions is yet another way in which adolescents become involved in the careful re-examination of the available tools of art-making – colour, form, texture, composition (Burton 1980; Specter 1987; Wolf 1988b).

As adolescents become capable of considering how to alter their own works to convey moods and messages, or to create specific effects, they become sensitive to similar efforts on the part of others. In this way, adolescents can approach the work of adult artists from a novel perspective. Not only can they read the surface of a painting to notice particular forms, materials or techniques, they can explore how these are matched to meanings. As compared with school-age children, adolescents can be engaged by what goes on 'behind the scenes' in works of art – by issues of symbolism, effects and double meanings. Thus adolescents, like the one quoted at the opening of this chapter, can begin to see the importance of knowing not just what the work 'is' but 'how' the painter, photographer or film-maker has chosen among avenues to make that work look as it does (Housen 1979; Machotka 1966; Parsons, Johnston and Durham 1978).

For adolescents who have the opportunity to go to museums, or at least to see reproductions, another major change occurs in the way that they look at works. They begin to have what could be called 'second sight'; they understand their own and others' work no longer as purely private enterprises but as building on and borrowing from one another. They begin to 'see' the historical, social or cultural side of art (Wolf 1988b).

These changes open up – maybe even burst open – the way students think about or reflect on art. They become aware that there are no absolute answers, no certain rules; they realize that different minds will construct different worlds and varying ways of evaluating those worlds (Chandler and Boyes 1982). 'Adolescents systematically shift the primary responsibility for the knowing process from the objects to the subjects of thought' (Chandler 1988: 409). Within the world of visual art that means there are no guarantees for making good paintings or for valuing one film far above another. In part this is exciting: many adolescents open up to the possibility that there are many kinds of 'good' in the world of art. But such a move can also bring a wash of doubts: high school art students can ask, if there is no certain better or worse, why bother to make art rather than tricks, why pay any more attention to paintings than to newspaper ads?

Out of these changes comes still a different kind of conversation about art-work. While the same three 'voices' are involved as were present for younger children, the concerns of each voice have evolved. As producers, high school students are less concerned with denotation or the rules of particular visual systems. Instead they are chiefly curious about how they might invent new systems or renditions. As perceivers, they notice much more than what is literally present on the paper or canvas: they can see symbols, effects and references to other works. As people who reflect on visual art they can wonder about its very basis.

Despite changes in the content of these stances, what remains critical is that artistic activity still involves an exchange between these points of view. Here a high school student speaks about the interplay between her own production and what she has perceived in other works (in this case a work of literature):

> I was reading a Greek play where the heroine, Deinira, becomes caught up in one tragedy after another ... she hangs herself from horror and grief. There's this idea of evil under everything. I got this idea of tangliness out of it ... When evil touches one part, it's everywhere. From that I began working on an image of a mythological creature with her hair tangled in the sun.
>
> (Cited in Wolf 1988b: 149)

Here another student describes her perception that there are many forms of success in the visual arts, highlighting how that insight affects her evaluations of her own productions:

When I look back over my portfolio, I realize there are lots of different kinds of success and failure there. I mean there is the success of a good idea, even if the image never lived up to it. There's the technical success of something really well-made. And there's the success of an image which is beautiful even if it doesn't mean something yet.

Conclusion

Even this brief look at the developmental changes in students' approaches to the visual arts shows that just as in the fields of reading or science, students at different ages have qualitatively different skills. Several illustrations will help to capture the qualities of these different periods. The illustrations come from a 6, a 9 and a 15 year old being asked to complete an already started drawing (a head and shoulders taken from the collection of Persian miniatures, *The Book of Kings*). What the 6 year old's drawing shows is a sensitivity to finishing a picture: the bottom of a body is supplied, the lines of the head and shoulders are carefully matched and continued. Missing, however, is any awareness of the particular kind of person depicted, or the set of artistic choices implied. By comparison, the 9 year old sees clues that his drawing must work within. He recognizes that drawings are particular systems or marks or connotations. Thus, when the 9 year old completes the Persian miniature drawing, he recognizes what he calls 'a fancy bad guy' and works within those implications, providing a costume, black moustache, medals, sword and boots. On a more formal plane, taking a cue from the head, the student systematically turns the torso and limbs as well. Finally, the adolescent appears to have an inkling that completing the figure calls for attention not only to what the figure is, but a set of artistic choices about *how it is rendered*. She completes it in a way that continues, not just the content or trappings, but the style – curving forms, fine lines, decorative detail. In this drawing there is attention to the particularly sinuous qualities of line, the composition of an overall pattern and the expression of fierceness through the asymmetry of the total composition.

Put in broader terms, in the preschool years children come to understand how a picture works, how it denotes objects, scenes, even imagined experience. In the middle years children recognize that there are fundamentally different kinds of visual systems, such as the sparse notational forms of maps and diagrams, the generic forms of dictionary illustrations and signs, the expressive and often idiosyncratic world of aesthetic images. In adolescence there comes a fascination with and an understanding of the concepts of choice, version and rendition.

But these are not stages in the usual sense of strategies which successively replace one another. Instead, they are more like points of inauguration. Each of these kinds of visual understanding, once initiated, continues to develop. What individuals are building is a vocabulary or a repertoire of ways of understanding visual codes. Even though it emerges early, our concern with the workings of denotation never goes away. The adolescent, for instance,

Figure 2.1 Completions of head and shoulders drawing by a 6 year old, a 9 year old and a 15 year old.

can think about an image as a picture, as an instance of a particular genre or system, and as an occasion for choice or rendition. The complexity of his or her understanding comes from having these multiple frames of reference. It is chiefly in this sense that later-occurring phases are 'better' rather than just qualitatively different.

Some caution ought to enter here. The descriptions offered here are based on average patterns of performance for just that segment of the American population which turns up in studies of child development. Until we have more diverse samples and considerable attention paid to individual patterns of growth, it will remain unclear whether we are looking at anything like universal, or even widely dispersed, patterns of aesthetic development. In America the efforts to teach children aesthetic skills have often in the past been short-term and underfunded, without much support from schools and communities. Under these circumstances, we cannot tell whether 7 year olds' inability to see the expressive or stylistic properties of paintings comes from some fundamental cognitive immaturity or from a failure to understand that these kinds of questions are relevant to paintings – a failure that comes from living in a world where interactions with works of visual art are few and sparse. The pattern could look quite different if it included Dutch children with their long histories of training in the arts and design or Arab nomad children whose material and cultural circumstances prevent them from drawing representational images. Until we have information about a wide range of children, we will not know whether the phases described are all that is possible, or only one rendition of what is possible.

But even as we need to broaden whose art work we consider, we also have to re-examine our familiar patterns for explaining aesthetic growth. Usually researchers and educators look to what might be called underlying factors – changes in eye-hand co-ordination, shifts in symbolic abilities, or the onset of schooling – to explain such qualitative shifts in children's art work. But, as the examples offered here suggest, we also ought to look 'internally', examining the interactions between the several stances which an individual often takes to visual experience: that of the producer, the perceiver and the reflective critic. Often one stance informs, challenges or supplements another, sparking changes in visual thinking.

The materials used here have come chiefly from the visual arts. But as the opening example of the young musician hints, the notion of art work as a conversation between stances, or differing forms of artistic knowledge, is not limited to the world of paintings and drawings. Similar conversations occur and inform work in music, dance and creative writing. Consider, for example, what this high school student says about the relationship between producing fiction and her capacity to understand the work of reading fiction:

> [I was writing a description of a room I had seen.] I had to read [it] out loud in class. Then people talked about it. One guy said he liked the way the writing had the feel of the room – jumbled and crowded. Someone else argued with him saying it was overdone. I was amazed. I knew I had

just written it off the top of my head. It put me on the inside looking out. It made me think that's what happens whenever you read. You are on the outside and you go hunting for clues; you find some, you invent others. But you don't find the original meaning just lying there; you build it up.

If this is indeed the case, there are strong implications for teaching and for research. If conversations between stances promote artistic development, then it becomes important to educate and promote rather than ignore or submerge that dialogue. Even students who are going to become painters or dancers (rather than art historians or critics) should have the chance to become skilled perceivers and thoughtful critics. This demands more than just opportunity. Young painters need avid debate and conversation about what they see, not just an entry card to museums. Young dancers need the experience of choreographing and engaging in criticism; it is not enough to learn the steps of someone else's dance or to be able to correct the steps in line with their vision of the dance. As researchers concerned with the course and quality of artistic growth, we need to put aside the traditional and, by now, comfortable separation between making, looking and thinking. We need to consider how we might overhear and understand the conversations that go on among these complementary capacities.

References

Brown, R. (1973). *A First Language*. Cambridge, Mass., Harvard University Press.

Burton, J. M. (1980). 'Line, space and the origins of meaning in human figure drawings made by children 8–15 years'. Unpublished doctoral thesis, Cambridge, Mass., Harvard University.

Carothers, T. and Gardner, H. (1979). 'When children's drawings become art: the emergence of aesthetic production and perception'. *Developmental Psychology*, 15(5): 570–80.

Chandler, M. J. (1988). 'Doubts and developing theories of mind', in J. Astington, P. Harris and D. Olson (eds.), *Developing Theories of Mind*. New York, Cambridge University Press.

Chandler, M. J. and Boyes, M. (1982). 'Social-cognitive development', in B. Wolman (ed.), *Handbook of Developmental Psychology*. Englewood Cliffs, NJ, Prentice-Hall.

Child, I. and Iwao, S. (1977). 'Young children's preferential responses to visual art'. *Scientific Aesthetics*, 1(14): 291–307.

Csikszentmihalyi, M. and Larson, R. (1984). *Being Adolescent*. New York, Basic Books.

Davidson, L. (1983). 'Early tonal structures in children's songs'. Paper presented at the International Conference on Psychology and the Arts, Cardiff, Wales.

Deloache, J., Strauss, M. and Maynard, J. (1979). 'Picture perception in infancy'. *Infant Behavior and Development*, 2: 77–89.

Deporter, D. and Kavanaugh, (1978). 'Parameters of children's sensitivity to painting styles'. *Studies in Art Education*, 20(1): 43–8.

Elkind, D. (1970). 'Developmental studies of figuration perception', in L. Lipsitt and

H. Reese (eds.), *Advances in Child Development and Behavior*, vol. 4. New York, Academic Press.

Erikson, E. (1963). *Childhood and Society*. New York, W. W. Norton.

(1968). *Youth, Identity, And Crisis*. New York, W. W. Norton.

Flavell, J., Green, R. and Flavell, E. (1986). 'Development of knowledge about the appearance–reality distinction'. *Monographs for the Society for Research in Child Development*. Chicago, University of Chicago Press.

Gardner, H. (1970). 'Children's sensitivity to painting styles'. *Child Development*, 41: 813–21.

(1973). *The Arts and Human Development*. New York, John Wiley.

(1983). *Frames of Mind*. New York, Basic Books.

Golomb, C. (1974). *Children's Painting and Sculpture*. Cambridge, Mass., Harvard University Press.

Hochberg, J. and Brooks, V. (1962). 'Pictorial recognition as an unlearned ability: a study of one child's performance'. *American Journal of Psychology*, 75: 624–8.

Housen, A. (1979). 'A review of studies of aesthetic understanding'. Special qualifying paper. Cambridge, Mass, Harvard University.

Jahoda, G., Deregowski, J., Ampene, E. and Williams, N. (1977). 'Pictorial recognition as an unlearned ability: a replication with children from pictorially deprived environments', in G. Butterworth (ed.), *The Child's Representation of the World*. New York, Plenum.

Kellogg, R. (1969). *Analyzing Children's Art*. Palo Alto, Calif., National Press Books.

Liben, L. and Downs, R. (1987). 'Maps as symbols'. Paper presented in the symposium 'Children's conceptions of maps as objects and representations'. Biennial Meeting of the Society for Research in Child Development, Baltimore, Md.

Lowenfeld, V. (1957). *Creative and Mental Growth*. New York, Macmillan.

Machotka, P. (1966). 'Aesthetic criteria in childhood: justifications of preference'. *Child Development*, 37: 877–85.

Nelson, K. (1986). *Event Knowledge*. Hillsdale, NJ, Lawrence Erlbaum Associates.

Parsons, M. (1987). *How We Understand Art*. Cambridge, Cambridge University Press.

Parsons, M., Johnston, M. and Durham, R. (1978). 'Developmental stages in children's aesthetic responses'. *Journal of Aesthetic Education*, 12(1): 83–104.

Rosenstiel, A., Morison, P., Silverman, J. and Gardner, H. (1978). 'Critical judgement: a developmental study'. *Journal of Aesthetic Education*, 12(4): 95–107.

Silverman, J., Winner, E., Rosenstiel, A. and Gardner, H. (1975). 'On training sensitivity to painting styles'. *Perception*, 4: 373–84.

Smith, N. R. (1972). 'The origins of graphic symbolization in children 3–5'. Ph.D. dissertation, Cambridge, Mass., Harvard University.

(1982). *Painting and Experience*. New York, Teachers College Press.

(1987). 'Drawing peppers'. Paper presented at the Annual Meeting of the American Psychological Association, New York, 28–31 August.

Specter, B. (1987). Comments in the panel discussion 'Discipline-based arts education in the '80's.' Carl Sandberg High School, Chicago, Ill.

Tizard, B. and Hughes, M. (1984). *Young Children Learning*. Cambridge, Cambridge University Press.

Walk. R. D. (1967). 'Concept formation and art: basic equipment and controls'. *Psychometric Science*, 9: 237–8.

Wellman, H. (1987). 'The young child's theory of mind'. Paper presented in the symposium 'The young child's concept of mind'. Biennial Meeting of the Society for Research in Child Development, Baltimore, Md.

Werner, H. and Kaplan, B. (1967). *Symbol Formation*. New York, John Wiley.

White, S. H. (1970). 'Some general outlines of the matrix of developmental changes between five and seven years'. *Bulletin of the Orton Society*, 20: 41–57.

Whiting, B. and Edwards, C. (1973). 'A cross-cultural analysis of sex differences in the behavior of children aged 3–11'. *Journal of Social Psychology*, 91: 171–88.

Willats, J. (1977). 'How children learn to represent three-dimensional space in drawings', in G. Butterworth (ed.), *The Child's Representation of the World*. New York, Plenum Press.

Wilson, B. (1974). 'The superheroes of J. C. Holtz: plus an outline of a theory of child art'. *Art Education*, November, pp. 2–9.

Wilson, B. and Wilson, M. (1977). 'An iconoclastic view of the imagery sources in the drawings of young people'. *Art Education*, 30: 33–42.

Winner, E. (1982). *Invented Worlds: The Psychology of the Arts*. Cambridge, Mass., Harvard University Press.

Winner, E., McCarthy, M., Kleinman, S. and Gardner, H. (1979). 'First metaphors', in D. Wolf (ed.), *Early Symbolization: New Directions for Child Development*, vol. 3.

Winner, E., Rosensteil, A. and Gardner, H. (1976). 'The development of metaphor understanding'. *Developmental Psychology*, 12: 289–97.

Wolf, D. (1984). 'Drawing conclusions about children's art'. Paper presented at 'Vom Kritzeln zur Kunst', Ichenhausen, Germany.

(1988a). 'Drawing the boundary', in J. Stiles-Davis and U. Bellugi (eds.), *The Development of Spatial Representation*. Hillsdale, NJ, Lawrence Erlbaum Associates.

(1988b). 'Artistic learning: what and where is it?' *Journal of Aesthetic Education*, 22(1): 143–55.

Wolf, D. and Gardner, H. (1980). 'Beyond playing and polishing', in J. E. Hausman (ed.), *Arts and the Schools*. New York, McGraw Hill.

Part II

Developments within artistic domains

3
Children's drawings

Maureen V. Cox

Children's drawings and paintings account for a large proportion of the material on the walls of playgroups, nurseries and school classrooms. Although it is acknowledged that children should have the opportunity to draw and paint – in order to develop their aesthetic sense, for instance – this experience is seen as incidental to the main business of the curriculum. It tends to be regarded as a pleasant, non-pressurized activity and one which may serve as a decorative adjunct or reward: 'You've done some very good number work. Now you can go and draw a picture.'

Drawing is rarely taught as a skill in its own right, particularly in the primary school. No one gets concerned if a child cannot produce a very good drawing by, say, the age of 11. We may have an *intuitive* idea of a good drawing and we may take note when a child seems particularly skilful, but we don't recommend remedial action if a child is not very good. This stands in stark contrast to reading, writing and number, where standards are much more clearly defined and remedial action is more readily offered.

Although certain kinds of art activity may be recommended for different age levels, there appear to be no formal, or even informal, criteria of an acceptable standard at each age. Many teachers judge children to be good or not good at drawing as if this is simply a matter of natural ability that they can't do anything about. Indeed, many people argue that we should not teach children how to draw, that to do so would be to interfere with the child's 'natural' self-expression and that such direct teaching would lead to an undesirable uniformity. It seems to me, however, that the teaching of basic skills in art would no more lead to uniformity in children's drawings than the teaching of letter formation, spelling and how to write in grammatical sentences leads to uniformity in their writing of stories and poems. In fact it is likely that if basic skills are withheld from children, they will be forced to rely on the stilted conventional forms which they happen to pick up in a haphazard way. In contrast, the teaching of drawing skills should free them from these conventions, enable them to observe objects and scenes more keenly and, as a consequence, lead them to produce fresher and more individualistic representations. Children are often dissatisfied with their own drawings, particularly at the age of about 9 onwards, and may become disheartened by the whole activity. They turn into adults who, if asked to draw, are embarrassed or dismissive about their lack of skill. It seems to me that we fail children if we do not at least attempt to help them towards acceptable solutions to their graphic problems.

I would certainly not want to take the fun out of drawing and turn it into a dull and onerous activity, but I think it is important to appreciate what making a representation actually involves. The artist, whether adult or child, must consider a number of problems and attempt to generate acceptable solutions to those problems. For example, we generally want to depict on a two-dimensional surface (a piece of paper) objects which, in the real world, exist in three dimensions. Now, three into two won't go. We can't draw the *whole* object, so we have to make decisions about which parts of it we will draw. Then, we have to decide what kind of mark best represents each feature, how these should be related to each other, and so on. The activity of drawing, then, is a problem-solving activity, as intellectually demanding as any other. Problem-solving, however, can also be fun.

The case of the missing torso

When children first wield a pencil or crayon they may not intend to draw a recognizable object at all. They simply enjoy the movement of the pencil or crayon and the making of marks on the paper. They discover that they can make different sorts of marks and experiment with these. Parents or teachers may suggest that the marks 'stand for' objects or people: 'Are you drawing Mummy?', 'Is this Daddy?'. These 'scribbles' will not be recognizable representations to the adult, and later the child probably won't recognize what she drew either. But gradually she comes to realize that other people expect her scribbles to represent something. It may also happen by chance that a child's scribble really does look like a person, a fish or a dog, and she recognizes this happy accident.

Some of the earliest children's drawings which adults *do* recognize and which children set out to construct deliberately are those of people. Human beings are quite complicated and the representation of them in a picture can also be tricky. Which bits of the body *must* we include and which bits are optional? What is an acceptable way of representing each bit? How are the bits related to each other or joined together?

Children's early attempts, around the age of 3 years, are undeniably peculiar. They are called *tadpole figures* in the jargon. Nearly all children draw them. These tadpole figures look peculiar because certain parts of the body appear to be missing and some features are attached to the body in a rather bizarre way. In particular, the tadpole seems to have no torso and, if arms are drawn at all, they seem to be attached to the head! Cox and Parkin

(1986) have also identified a 'transitional' figure which some children draw before going on to conventional forms (Fig. 3.1). Although the transitional form, like the tadpole, has only one closed contour, its body features (arms, tummy button, etc.) are placed lower on the figure.

There are different ideas about why children draw tadpole figures. Some people (e.g. Gibson 1969) think that young children have an incomplete

Tadpole figures have a single enclosed contour, usually containing facial features. Arms are frequently omitted. If they are included, they are attached to the closed unit.

In *transitional figures*, body features such as arms, navel and buttons, are drawn on the lower part of the figure.

Conventional figures usually have separate head and body contours. Occasionally the whole figure is outlined with one contour.

Figure 3.1   Young children's drawings of the human figure.

mental image of the human body, that the torso in particular is missing, and is subsequently omitted from their drawings. It could be the case, however, that their image is complete but that they choose to include in their drawings only those body parts which are significant to them and, for some reason, that the torso is not among these.

There are other researchers (e.g. Freeman 1975, 1980) who believe that the child's mental image is complete but that excessive production problems result in omissions from the actual drawing. In Freeman's view, then, the tadpole figure lacks a body which is present in the mental image. We know that children tend to scan objects along a vertical axis from top to bottom (Ghent 1961; Howard and Templeton 1966) and that they tend to draw body parts in this order too. From the research on memory (e.g. Glanzer and Cunitz 1966) we know that there is a tendency to recall correctly the items first and last on a list but to forget items in the middle. In the activity of drawing, not only must the child recall all the body parts, but this must be done in the appropriate order; furthermore, there are other pressing demands such as how each part should be drawn and how the parts should be fixed together. We would expect, then, that the task demands would lead to omissions, and that the torso, being in the middle of the list of body parts to be drawn, would be a most likely candidate for omission.

There are yet other researchers (e.g. Paget 1932; Arnheim 1975) who agree that the child's body image is complete, but who argue that the torso is actually included in the tadpole drawing. Their point is that the young child does not segment the body image into such detailed parts as do older children and adults. It could be that the single closed contour of the tadpole encompasses the mass of the figure – that is the head and the body – and then the arms and legs are appended to it. On the other hand, it could be that the torso is located beneath the 'head' contour and between the 'legs' of the figure.

It is not necessarily the case, of course, that all tadpoles 'mean' the same thing. Some children certainly say that their figure has no body because 'I can't draw bodies'. Others assert vehemently that their figure does have a body and can tell you exactly where it is. I set out to ask children about their tadpole drawings (Cox, in preparation). There were ninety-three tadpole drawers in all, aged between 3 years and 4 years 6 months. Since children are not familiar with the term 'torso' and because we were worried about the possible ambiguity of the term 'body' (i.e. it could refer to the torso or to the whole person), we talked about the 'body' with forty-six of the children and 'tummy' with forty-seven of them. In fact all of them pointed to their torsos when asked to indicate their own body/tummy. All of the children, except four, said that there was a body/tummy in their drawing. The vast majority said that it was in the lower part of the closed contour; a small minority located the body/tummy between the 'legs'. All the children except one drew a tummy button on their figure; the majority drew it in the lower part of the closed contour.

These results support the view of Paget and Arnheim that the tadpole figure does have a torso but that this is not clearly differentiated from other body parts. For most children, the closed contour represents both the head and the body of the figure. This means that when children attach arms to this contour, their figure is not so bizarre as at first it might appear; the arms are not necessarily attached to the head at all, but to the body. It should be emphasized that this lack of differentiation of head and body does not necessarily apply to the children's perception and understanding of a real human figure, since they are quite capable of identifying a person's head and torso; the lack of differentiation is at the level of representation.

Whereas some children have a very short tadpole 'stage', others may carry on drawing them for many months (Cox and Parkin 1986). You may in fact find some tadpole-drawers in infant classes. But children do not go on drawing tadpoles forever. Eventually they come under pressure, usually from other children, to adopt the more conventional form for the human figure.

Identifying the body

How can we best encourage children to draw a more conventional representation of the human figure? So far, we have found two methods which work quite well; there may, of course, be more. The first is very teacher-directed. It is basically a copying task, copying a conventional figure drawing (Cox and Samuels, in preparation). The teacher asks the child to watch while she draws a head on her piece of paper and then invites the child to draw a head on his. Next, the teacher draws in the body on her figure, and the child draws in the body on his. This procedure is followed for all the body parts the teacher wishes to include. It is advisable to stick to a fairly simple figure, including, say, head and facial features, body, arms and legs. It is also advisable to name and talk about the different parts as they are drawn. We have found that it is better to do several drawings like this, perhaps representing different members of the child's family or friends, rather than one single drawing. It is also important that the child watches while the teacher draws one part, and then draws the equivalent part on his own figure. This step-by-step procedure is effective, whereas simply asking the child to copy a pre-drawn conventional figure or asking him to watch while the teacher draws the whole figure before he tries to copy it, does not produce lasting results.

The other method of promoting more conventional forms is much less teacher-directed. It really amounts to dropping a very heavy hint that the head and body should be drawn as two separate forms. Annie Trapp (Cox and Trapp, in preparation) asked children to draw a person who has a purple head and a green body (or vice versa). A purple and a green crayon were provided. We also showed them a figure, modelled out of Fimo modelling medium, with appropriately coloured head and body parts, so that both visual and verbal cues were available. Under these conditions, 70 per cent of tadpole-drawers drew a more advanced figure. A few children drew a transitional figure (24 per cent), but most drew a conventional form (76 per cent). We were interested to know which cues were the most important, visual or verbal. Another group of tadpole-drawers was tested: half of them (the visual group) were asked to draw the model figure which they saw in front of them; the other half (the verbal group) had no model to look at but were asked to draw a person with a purple head and a green body. We found that it was the verbal group which did better, in that they produced more advanced drawings; the majority of the visual group produced their usual tadpole form. This may seem surprising, but our observations of the children's behaviour make it clear what was going on. The children in the verbal condition often repeated the instructions and this seemed to guide them through the task. In contrast, the children in the visual group paid little attention to the model figure; even though the purple and green crayons had been placed alongside the same-colour body parts of the model, these visual cues were obviously not explicit enough to direct the children's attention to the head–body distinction. It seems that the model served only to cue the children to draw their usual human figure form, namely a tadpole.

Draw it like it is

Very young children are probably not terribly concerned whether or not other people recognize what their drawings are supposed to represent. By the time they go to school, however, they are concerned that their drawings should be recognizable, and they pick up conventional and stylized ways of drawing things. Their drawings of different houses may look very similar, for example, even though the actual houses differ very markedly. Children who live in a terraced street or a centrally heated block of flats very often draw their 'own' detached house, complete with smoking chimney. Even if they do add particular features in order to identify a specific object, they seem to show no concern about how it would look from a particular viewpoint. Consequently, their drawings often include parts of objects that simply cannot be seen in reality. The drawings of children in the early and middle years of the primary school, then, include recognizable and stylized items, but they rarely reflect any concern for photographic realism.

Take, for example, a cup. Cups usually have handles. If you ask young children (say between the ages of 5 and 7) to draw a picture of a cup, they will draw it with a handle at the side. If you place a real cup in front of them and turn it so that the handle is out of sight and ask them to draw *this* cup as it looks from where they are sitting, they will still draw a cup complete with handle (Freeman and Janikoun 1972; Davis 1983). Children seem to be intent on making their drawing identifiable. Without the handle the drawing simply does not look like a cup. My daughter, aged 4 years 11 months, drew the 'bowl' of a cup which I had placed in front of her, its handle turned away. She looked at the cup and at her drawing. She then drew a handle attached to the right-hand side of the cup saying, 'I can't see the handle, but I'm going to draw it anyway. It makes it look better.'

In order to draw objects as they appear from a particular point of view, we often have to sacrifice important information which may be crucial in identifying what the object is supposed to be, and children may be reluctant to do this.

A drawing which captures the way the object looks from a certain viewpoint is called a *viewer-centred* picture. In contrast, a picture which concentrates on factual information about the object, independently of the way it happens to look, is called an *object-centred* picture (Marr 1982). Younger children tend to draw object-centred pictures whereas older children and adults tend to draw, although not always successfully, viewer-centred pictures. Some researchers like Luquet (1913, 1927) and Piaget (Piaget and Inhelder 1956, 1969) regard the change as a developmental shift reflecting greater cognitive maturity; other researchers (e.g. Hagen 1985, 1986) see the different representations as a choice that the 'artist' makes reflecting different intentions and criteria.

Let's take another example, this time an object like a table or a cube. Tables generally have rectangular tops, and cubes, by definition, have six faces which are all squares. If we were to look at a real table, the top would only look rectangular if we viewed it directly from above or directly from below. Normally, a table top appears as some form of trapezium or trapezoid shape. If you stand in front of a table the far edge appears shorter than the near edge and the sides seem to converge with distance. Similarly, with a cube, we can only see a face of the cube as square if we place that face directly in front of our eyes; no other face of the cube would then be visible. If we turn the cube so that more faces of the cube can be seen (no more than three), none of the faces appears to be square; they are all trapezoidal (Fig. 3.2).

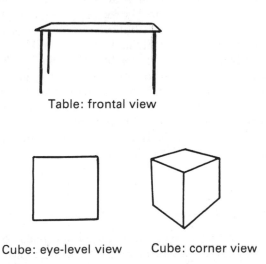

Table: frontal view

Cube: eye-level view   Cube: corner view

Figure 3.2   Examples of a table and a cube drawn 'in perspective'.

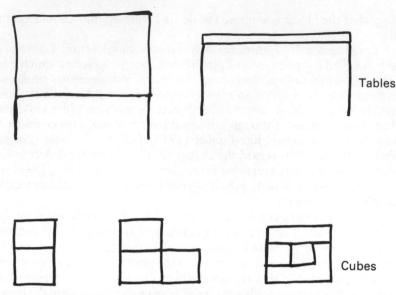

Figure 3.3   Young children's drawings of a table and a cube.

In order to draw these objects as they appear we have to sacrifice important information about them. The table top and the faces of the cube are not drawn as rectangles even though we know that the real objects are rectangular. The drawings of children up to about 9 years, however, are usually rectilinear, that is the surfaces are drawn as rectangles (Willats 1977; Mitchelmore 1978; Freeman 1980; Cox 1986a, 1986b) (Fig. 3.3).

Not only do we have this conflict between appearance and reality when we are trying to draw a *single* object, but we also have a problem in relating different objects within a scene. If we look at, say, a still life, some parts of the scene may be totally or partially hidden by other objects which are nearer to the viewer. We know that the whole of each object actually exists, yet if we are to draw what we see, we must omit the hidden parts.

If you arrange a very simple scene, say one ball in front of, and partially masking, another, and ask children between the ages of 4 and 7 to draw it, most of them will draw both balls complete and arranged separately, one above the other (Cox 1978, 1981) (Fig. 3.4).

'I'm not very good at drawing'

Young children have a relatively uninhibited approach to drawing. They sometimes say they can't draw something – they don't know 'how it goes' – but generally they get on with it in a bold and unselfconscious way. On the whole, children choose their own subject-matter and plan their own pictures

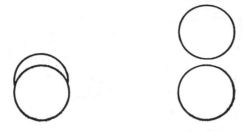

Figure 3.4 The viewer sees that one ball partially occludes the other, but the child draws them separately.

without reference to the spatial problems that confront artists when trying to squeeze three dimensions into two. Rarely, if ever, are children given a drawing task which sets out to tax their problem-solving capabilities in a pictorial context.

In our culture the adoption of a particular viewpoint is taken as the norm, and, by the age of about 9, children set themselves this viewer-centred criterion for judging their own efforts and those of others. They want their picture of a house to resemble the actual house it is supposed to represent. Their portrait of mum or dad should look like mum and dad, not like any woman or man. They want to make objects, like tables and buildings, appear three-dimensional. The result is that older primary school children start getting dissatisfied with their pictures. They begin to recognize that their efforts cannot match the standards they wish to attain. They are often less bold and more meticulous, and do a lot of rubbing out. This is the time when children may welcome some tuition in *how* to draw. But very often we, as teachers and parents, cannot help either because we haven't got the skills ourselves or because we feel that we would be interfering with the child's free self-expression if we taught a particular way of drawing something.

The example I gave earlier of my daughter's drawing of a cup suggests that quite young children are sometimes aware of the conflict between their knowledge of a scene, and of how it looks from one viewpoint. I suspect, though, that this conflict is rarely made explicit. Whereas adults have learnt that the instructions 'draw what you see' or 'draw how it looks from here' are directing them to the actual visual appearance of the object (a viewer-centred picture), children may not interpret the instructions in the same way. They may assume that the adult's instructions are directing their attention to the *identity* of the object. This is likely to bias them towards an object-centred representation, such that they do not even consider the possibility of a viewer-centred representation.

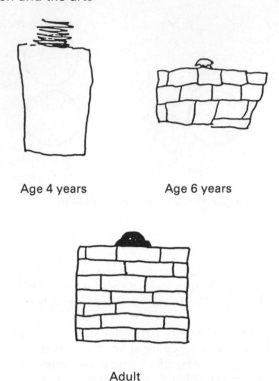

Age 4 years   Age 6 years

Adult

Figure 3.5   Viewer-centred pictures of a robber hiding behind a wall.

Teaching children to draw what they see

There is some evidence that children do not necessarily draw object-centred pictures. Various research studies demonstrate that children as young as 6, and sometimes even as young as 4 or 5, will attempt to make their drawing look like the particular view they have of an object or a scene. This suggests that children much younger than the age of 9 could usefully be given guidance in how to draw what they see.

Let's go back to the example of a cup. If children are asked to draw a single cup with its handle turned out of sight, they nevertheless include a handle in their drawing. Alyson Davis (1983, 1985) presented children with *two* cups, one with its handle to the side and one with its handle turned away. The two cups were identical except for their orientation. The children had no difficulty in drawing this scene as it looked, that is with the handle omitted from one cup. Davis argued that there was no ambiguity about the identity of the two objects – they were both cups. In order to distinguish between them and to emphasize the difference in orientation, the children were willing to leave out the handle. Thus, by manipulating the context, the child can be led towards a viewer-centred solution to the task.

Recently, with the help of Marianne Hare, I have asked children aged between 4 years 6 months and 6 years 6 months to draw a series of pictures of a single cup. The cup was systematically rotated in front of some of the children, whereas others were asked to occupy different chairs around the table in order to obtain different views of the cup. We found that both groups of children understood that the task was about the different orientations of the cup and had no difficulty in drawing these, readily omitting the handle when it was not visible.

I have also manipulated the context when asking children to draw an integrated scene (Cox 1981, 1986a). Remember that when asked to draw two objects, one partly obscuring another, children usually draw two complete and separate objects. I set up a scene in which a robber was hiding behind a wall. Unfortunately for the robber, a policeman could see the top of his head over the wall; the children were asked to draw what the policeman could see. Six year olds, and even many 4 year olds, had no difficulty in drawing a viewer-centred picture with only the man's head peeping over the wall (Fig. 3.5).

Another, perhaps more explicit, way of bringing children's attention to the appearance of a scene is to ask them to point out the parts that can be seen and the parts that can't. Alison Bowes and I (Cox and Bowes, in preparation) showed 7 year olds a blue ball behind a red one. They were invited to talk about these and to indicate verbally, as well as by pointing, the parts of the blue ball that could and could not be seen. When we looked at their drawings of the balls, we found that more of these children drew viewer-centred pictures than did another group of the same age who had simply been asked to draw the scene as it looked from where they were sitting. A third group was provided with an extra cue in the scene, in that the lower half of the blue ball was in this case painted yellow. The distinct colour difference between the visible (blue) and hidden (yellow) parts of the farther ball gave rise to an even higher proportion of children in this group who drew viewer-centred pictures. Although this method worked well with 7 year olds, we found that it did not help 5 year olds to draw viewer-centred pictures; they drew both balls separately regardless of the instruction.

In order to draw a cup with its handle turned out of sight, in a viewer-centred way, children have only to omit the handle; they do not have to alter the drawing in any positive kind of way. In contrast, in order to draw a viewer-centred picture of the robber partially occluded by a wall or a ball partially occluded by another ball, they must not only omit part of the masked object but also join the outer contour of the farther object to the contour of the nearer one with 'junctions'. Some children can draw the visible part of the farther object, but have not learnt how to use junctions (Fig. 3.6). They may draw a complete contour around the visible part and set it either adjacent to or even apart from the contour of the nearer object. Thus in some children's pictures of these scenes you may see a scalp 'sitting' on a wall or even 'floating' above the wall, and a half-moon part of a ball similarly 'hovering' in the air (Cox 1985) (Fig. 3.6). These children may be unfamiliar

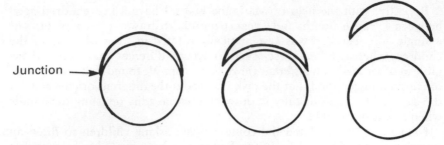

Junction

Figure 3.6   Different methods of drawing one ball partially occluded by another.

with the conventional use of junctions simply because they have never been presented with an occlusion problem and have therefore never had cause even to consider a solution. If children don't use junctions spontaneously, they can easily be shown how.

Getting children to omit a discrete part of an object, such as a cup handle is

Figure 3.7   Stylized picture of a cube 'in depth'.

relatively easy: in the studies mentioned earlier, we have found that 5 and 6 year olds can manage it. Children can also omit from their drawings the part of an object which is masked by a nearer object in the scene. Although the age at which they can do this seems to depend on the kinds of objects in the scene and the instructions given, by the age of 7 years most children are successful.

What is of interest here is whether or not the children can omit from their drawings the part of the scene which is hidden. We have not been concerned with *how* the visible parts of the scene have been drawn – for instance, whether or not the shape of the cup in the drawing matches that in the scene. It may be a great problem for children to draw the perceived shape of the visible parts of objects. Let's take the example of an object such as a table or a cube which typically have rectangular surfaces. The successful viewer-centred representation of the 'depth' of a table or a cube tends to be defined by the way the surfaces are drawn. If seen from the front, the perceived shape of the table-top is a trapezium even though its actual shape is a rectangle. The issue is not simply one of omitting part of the table or cube, but of drawing the visible faces in a particular way. Up to about the age of 9, as we saw earlier, children draw rectilinear forms to represent these objects. By the age of 12 most of them have been taught to draw a cube 'in depth' (Fig. 3.7), and they will generalize this to tables. They are often told that this is how to draw 'in perspective'.

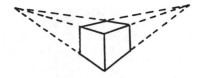

Figure 3.8   A perspective projection of a cube.

If a cube is placed in this 'corner' orientation, no face can be seen as a rectangle and none of the pairs of opposite sides as parallel (Fig. 3.8). In fact, these stylized forms taught to children are not viewer-centred pictures or perspective drawings at all.

I placed a cube on a table and positioned it so that only the front and top faces could be seen, and asked 7 year olds and adults to draw it. Although more adults than children converged the edges of the top face, the majority in both groups drew rectilinear forms (Cox 1986a, 1986b). The problem is that it is very difficult to 'see' that the edges of the top face appear to converge, especially when you know that in fact they are parallel.

The problem for the teacher, then, is how to help children to 'see' the shape of the objects. It is very unlikely that anyone would ever begin to draw 'in perspective' simply by looking closely at objects. Of course, we do have to look at objects if we are to draw them. But the 'trick' is to see them not as three-dimensional objects but as two-dimensional shapes. The artist must inhibit the tendency to see three-dimensional objects and, instead, must imagine their projections onto a two-dimensional surface. Leonardo da Vinci, who formulated the laws of perspective, compared this to holding up a pane of glass between the artist and the scene; maintaining a fixed viewpoint, the artist traces around the shapes seen through the glass. There are many illustrations of devices designed to help artists do just this (Fig. 3.9).

Presumably with practice, artists learn to manage without such physical props; and no doubt some people manage without them to start with. Drawing in perspective is not something that develops automatically with maturity; it is not a 'natural' thing to do. It is an 'artful' technique which is acquired, and so this aspect of drawing needs *particular* tuition.

There are, of course, books (e.g. Edwards 1979; Woods 1984) and art courses which are designed to teach people how to draw, but usually these are taken up by children and adults who have already shown an interest and aptitude. It seems to me quite likely that ordinary children could improve their drawing skills using similar techniques. One very simple exercise is to ask children to draw on the window with a washable felt-tip pen. They should close one eye, try to maintain a fixed position, while tracing round the buildings and objects they see through the glass. Obviously, considerable concentration and co-ordination are needed so that this activity is most appropriate for children around the age of 10 years, although I dare say, some well-motivated younger children could achieve good results.

You could also construct a 'viewing box' from a large cardboard or

Figure 3.9   Perspective frame. Albrecht Dürer, *Der Zeichner des liegenden Weibes*, woodcut (B. 149). (Reprinted with permission of Kupferstichkabinett Staatliche Museen Preussicher Kulturbesitz, Berlin.)

wooden box: a transparent piece of glass or perspex is substituted for one of the short ends of the box, and the opposite end and top are cut away. A scene can be arranged in the box and the artist can draw on the glass panel. Then, place a sheet of paper on the glass and trace over the lines; illumination from a torch held behind the glass is useful. Finally, the lines can be wiped off the glass ready for another drawing.

Conclusion

Most young children enjoy drawing. Although we see this as an important experience for them, we do not rate it highly enough to warrant direct tuition in drawing techniques. Indeed, we seem intent on keeping drawing at the level of self-expression, with little aspiration towards 'art', in the communicative sense. Consequently, when enthusiastic young children grow older, many have acquired very little in the way of drawing skills and may be disenchanted with their efforts.

I have heard it argued that the formal teaching of drawing skills would stifle children's imagination and lead to a uniformity of style. In this chapter, I have tried to show, with the aid of just a few examples, that it is precisely the lack of tuition which leads both children and adults to rely on stylized pictorial forms. Tuition need not mean the teaching of a set formula for each particular object; rather, it involves the observation of objects in all possible orientations. Far from stifling the imagination, tuition can help liberate it. Even the greatest artists have served a period of apprenticeship in which they have studied and absorbed the techniques which have gone before them. Innovation is generally based on a firm mastery of basic techniques.

References

Arnheim, R. (1975). *Art and Visual Perception*. 2nd edn. Berkeley, Calif., University of California Press.

Cox, M. V. (1978). 'Spatial depth relationships in young children's drawings'. *Journal of Experimental Child Psychology*, 26: 551–4.

  (1981). 'One thing behind another: problems of representation in children's drawings'. *Educational Psychology*, 1: 275–87.

  (1985). 'One object behind another: young children's use of array-specific or view-specific representations', in N. H. Freeman and M. V. Cox (eds.), *Visual Order: The Nature and Development of Pictorial Representation*. Cambridge, Cambridge University Press.

  (1986a). *The Child's Point of View: The Development of Cognition and Language*. Brighton, Harvester Press.

  (1986b). 'Cubes are difficult things to draw'. *British Journal of Developmental Psychology*, 4: 341–5.

  (in preparation). 'Young children's drawings of the human figure: the case of the missing torso'.

Cox, M. V. and Bowes, A. (in preparation). 'Children's drawings of one object behind another: the effects of identifying the visible and nonvisible parts of the scene'.

Cox, M. V. and Parkin, C. E. (1986). 'Young children's human figure drawing: cross-sectional and longitudinal studies'. *Educational Psychology*, 6: 353–68.

Cox, M. V. and Samuels, T. (in preparation). 'Teaching "tadpole"-drawers to draw conventional human figures'.

Cox, M. V. and Trapp, A (in preparation). 'Human figure drawings: the effect of visual and verbal cues on "tadpole"-drawers'.

Davis, A. M. (1983). 'Contextual sensitivity in young children's drawings'. *Journal of Experimental Child Psychology*, 35: 478–86.

  (1985). 'The canonical bias: young children's drawings of familiar objects', in N. H. Freeman and M. V. Cox (eds.), *Visual Order: The Nature and Development of Pictorial Representation*. Cambridge, Cambridge University Press.

Edwards, B. (1979). *Drawing on the Right Side of the Brain: A Course in Enhancing Creativity and Artistic Confidence*. Los Angeles, J. P. Tarcher.

Freeman, N. H. (1975). 'Do children draw men with arms coming out of the head?' *Nature*, 254: 416–17.

  (1980). *Strategies of Representation in Young Children*. London, Academic Press.

Freeman, N. H. and Janikoun, R. (1972). 'Intellectual realism in children's drawings of a familiar object with distinctive features'. *Child Development*, 43: 1116–21.

Ghent, L. (1961). 'Form and its orientation: a child's eye-view'. *American Journal of Psychology*, 74: 177–90.

Gibson, E. J. (1969). *Principles of Perceptual Learning and Development*. New York, Appleton-Century-Crofts.

Glanzer, M. and Cunitz, A. R. (1966). 'Two storage mechanisms in free recall'. *Journal of Verbal Learning and Verbal Behavior*, 5: 351–60.

Hagen, M. A. (1985). 'There is no development in art', in N. H. Freeman and M. V. Cox (eds.), *Visual Order: The Nature and Development of Pictorial Representation*. Cambridge, Cambridge University Press.

  (1986). *Varieties of Realism: Geometries of Representational Art*. Cambridge, Cambridge University Press.

Howard, I. P. and Templeton, W. B. (1966). *Human Spatial Orientation*. Chichester, Wiley.

Luquet, G. H. (1913). *Les Dessins d'un enfant*. Paris, Alcan.

  (1927). *Le Dessin enfantin*. Paris, Alcan.

Marr, D. (1982). *Vision: A Computational Investigation of Visual Representation in Man*. San Francisco, Freeman.

Mitchelmore, M. C. (1978). 'Developmental stages in children's representations of regular solid figures'. *Journal of Genetic Psychology*, 133: 229–39.

Paget, G. W. (1932). 'Some drawings of men and women made by children of certain non-European races'. *Journal of the Royal Anthropological Institute*, 62: 127–44.

Piaget, J. and Inhelder, B. (1956). *The Child's Conception of Space*. London, Routledge & Kegan Paul.

(1969). *The Psychology of the Child*. London, Routledge & Kegan Paul.

Willats, J. (1977). 'How children learn to represent three-dimensional space in drawings', in G. Butterworth (ed.), *The Child's Representation of the World*. New York, Plenum Press.

Woods, M. (1984). *Perspective in Art*. London, Batsford.

4
Education and development in music from a cognitive perspective

Lyle Davidson and Larry Scripp

A cognitive-developmental model of music education

There is currently a lack of consensus among researchers and educators about what musical development might be. Researchers typically prefer experimental designs which model development in single modalities outside of musical instruction. Classroom teachers see only the slice of development which occurs during limited time periods. Private instrumental teachers, on the other hand, trace performance ability through many years, yet often fail to see the development of musical abilities outside of performance skills.

Imagining an institution where teachers and researchers could share their observations of a complete range of musical development, its laboratories would have to feature examples of musical instruction, practice and creative growth that takes place from early infancy to adulthood, from the musical novice to the expert practitioner. On the ground floor, for example, we observe children learning or inventing songs at their mother's knee. In another wing, experimenters test very young children's ability to discriminate between bells of various pitches and use them to play back songs they know. On the floors immediately above, researchers study children's first Suzuki violin classes or watch children write out music with their own invented symbol systems. Near the top floor, conservatory-level music theory and master classes are being observed, while, taking advantage of modern technology, we may observe trained and untrained adolescents and adults composing with the support of a computer.

Although it is easy to observe these diverse activities, it is more demanding to think of a framework which integrates such diversity. It is difficult to learn about musical development and music cognition from observing individual centres of this laboratory in isolation. For example, one's understanding of children's musical knowledge is handicapped by not being aware of the end-states of such knowledge, just as one's understanding of adults' knowledge of music is incomplete without knowing its beginnings. The questions below attempt to draw together issues which need to be kept in mind as our story unfolds.

First, what mode of musical knowledge are we going to investigate: perception, performance, composition or representation? Emphasizing musical knowledge in terms of skill, we will focus primarily on the development and control of performance and problem-solving expertise. Accordingly, our view of musical growth will focus on how individuals use their musical knowledge to solve composition problems, performance problems, or represent music with novel or conventional graphic symbols.

Second, under what conditions of training are we going to look for musical development? We will consider four conditions: children and adults without musical training, and children and adults with musical training. Taking all of these conditions into account, we can investigate the interaction of types of musical knowledge with degrees of training. This produces a four-cell matrix for investigating perception, performance, composition and representation. With this approach, teachers can be informed of musical development that occurs outside the condition of music instruction. Research articulating the developmental sequences of untrained children may, for example, better describe the context or effects of instruction.

Third, the musical validity of the context of the problem being investigated or the lesson being taught follows closely on the issue of degree of training. The contexts across which musical cognition and development can be observed vary greatly, from despairingly lean to overwhelmingly rich. At one extreme, experimental studies of music perception may present a small number of tones with minimal musical content or context; at the other extreme, identifying, specifying and modelling (in any significant way) the memory, motor and interpretative skills of a practising professional musician challenges even the most experienced observer (Blum 1986; Schon 1987). Stressing the common ground between education and psychology, we will present examples of research findings that contribute to the understanding of skill development in the rehearsal studio or classroom.

Finally, do traditional music pedagogies contribute to our understanding of musical cognition? It is possible to view everyday teaching practice as part of a programme of empirical research. It is also possible to assess the support provided by different traditional pedagogical systems in terms of musical cognitive development. However, once the underlying assumptions and stances of various pedagogical systems are analysed, we may be faced with conflicting assumptions about musical development and learning. For example, to some teachers, learning to sing, to play the violin or to compose is predominantly a matter of ensuring that the naturally creative and curious child has ample opportunity for expression; to others, learning consists of repeating steps leading to the mastery of a given lesson or skill, while to yet others, learning is reflected in a student's ability to solve increasingly complex problems independently. Our attitude toward these three points of view will greatly determine our approach to understanding development and education.

The premises of contemporary educational practice may be observed from three different perspectives of development (Kohlberg and Mayer 1972). From the *maturational* view, the individual child has a set of desirable traits which must be allowed to unfold and undesirable traits which must be brought under control; from the *cultural transmission* view, the increasingly socialized child receives conventional valued skills and knowledge as presented by the culture; and finally, from the *cognitive- developmental* view, the individual maturing child is seen interacting with a structured environment – interactions which both stimulate and trace the increasingly complex cognitive transformations of the developing child.

Each of these views contains distinct tendencies which play central roles in designing educational processes, procedures and evaluations. The maturationist theory, valuing the presence of desirable traits or skills in the child, avoids the use of rote learning, drills and other highly structured practices because they impose the values of others on the child. Learning, for the maturationist, consists of being able to express one's understanding and control one's behaviour. Applied to music, this theory favours programmes which allow the child maximum opportunity to exercise creative impulses and suggests that the child may suffer from untimely introduction of pedagogical interventions or inflexible programmes and conventions.

Consider the case of young children's development of music notation skills. From the maturational point of view, children might be encouraged to invent their own notational systems as they perceive the need for conveying their musical ideas. At some point they may choose to adopt the conventional music notation system of the culture. With self-taught musicians, this need may never arise.

In contrast, the cultural transmission model relies on rote learning, drills and other highly structured methods of practice. For this child, school is the place where one internalizes the skills and knowledge of the culture. In this model of cultural transmission, learning occurs as the continuous accumulation of cultural information or skill. Since children have to learn the conventional notation system in order to be musically literate, they start with the conventional graphic elements they are taught and add new symbols until the system is complete. A notation task is a test of their knowledge of the standard notation system.

Finally, the cognitive-developmental model places the highest value on the interactions of the individual within the environment. Instructional environments purposefully place the child in situations of conflict. Learning occurs with the development of problem-solving strategies required for resolving cognitive conflicts in the environment. We see the child solving musical problems through inventive means. For the cognitive-developmentalist, learning results in active change in patterns of thinking which unfold with cognitive development.

The viewpoint toward education plays a vital role in our agenda of exploring the growth of rich problem-solving expertise in the context of our musical culture. Adopting the cognitive-developmental view, we control for individual training and unfolding development as independent variables in musical development. This educational perspective stresses the importance of mapping the developmental paths that children and adults reveal in relatively natural settings.

Whatever developmental paths we may find are probably not smooth. Most educators would probably agree with psychologists that musical development occurs in fits and starts. Despite constant interactions with the teacher or environment, long periods of practice tend to be followed by a suddenly marked improvement in ability. Psychologists observe (while teachers hope) that such changes lead to periods during which new abilities and behaviours become relatively stable, and are characterized by thought processes which are qualitatively different from those of the preceding period. This structural orientation to development is based on the premise that change occurs in alternating phases of stability and instability. Developmental stages tend to progress in invariant sequences, marking qualitatively different cognitive structures. Since both educators and psychologists observe periods of relative stability that characteristically alternate with relatively rapid periods of growth and change, we argue for the integration of the developmental framework as a way to reconsider musical development – with or without training.

For example, a cognitive-developmental model for teaching music notation will take a radically different approach from the other perspectives. Carefully structured problems stimulate the child to invent and refine solutions which draw on their level of cognitive development. This approach uses what the child brings to the task and present lessons in a sequence which mirrors more clearly the path of the child's natural development. From this point of view, the teacher can design a curriculum which makes use of children's capacity to invent notations by introducing the concepts and practice of notation in the order of appearance identified through systematic observation.

Recent research provides us with the background for just such a model. Close analysis of children's notations (Davidson and Scripp 1988a) or compositions (Swanwick and Tillman 1986) suggests that, although few of the children use standard musical symbols, their changing representations or performances reflect an ordered set of qualitatively different levels of musical understanding. This sequence can inform teachers about levels of understanding possible without the use of conventional symbols or musical training.

Cognitive frameworks underlying musical development

In this section we will attempt to adapt specific models of cognitive development to the domain of music. Looking at a wide range of musical examples we see the need for frameworks that help articulate this point of view. At first, we will use Bruner's stages of early representational processes to demonstrate and sketch out the initial levels of musical thinking (Bruner 1973). Later, we will use Fischer's (1980) model of skill theory to describe the increasingly complex formations of musical cognition across a range of performance and representational contexts (Fischer and Pipp 1984). Finally broad frameworks based on the work of Piaget (1983) and Vygotsky (1978) will be employed to buttress the notion of development in composition and improvisation. Having established the theoretical underpinnings, we will then identify frameworks drawn from the psychological research in music that suggest discrete and invariant levels of musical cognition with and without musical training.

Considering representations as selected stable knowledge across many dimensions, Bruner (1973) offers three kinds of representational processes based upon *motor actions, images* and *language systems*. These representations express qualitatively different types of knowledge ranging from the first sensory-motor responses to fully functioning symbol systems. According to Bruner, the more advanced symbolic representations enrich rather than replace the initial action oriented stages, just as even though we now walk upright, we retain our ability to crawl.

While Bruner's chief concern is with early cognitive development, we see broad implications for interactions of musical performance and notation suggested by this framework. As symbol systems are invented or learnt, the more enactive representations are increasingly dimensionalized. As the bowings and fingerings of the violin are incorporated in notation, the enactive mode is no less important in performance, but new cognitive structures are now called into play. Articulation can be conceived and organized by symbolic manipulation or by enactive demonstration by the master teacher.

Research in young children's musical representations (Bamberger 1986; Davidson and Scripp 1988a; Upitis 1987) shows striking support for this concept of cognitive growth. In Bruner's terms, children first use enactive scribbles that capture the action of the piece – to trace rhythmic or structural features of the song. Although their feelings of musical pulse or rhythm may have been co-ordinated with the scribbles, little can be read back by the children. Later on, children are more apt to use images to represent the song. In our example, a 6 year old uses a rebus or a string of icons to capture the lyrics, storyline and rhythmic pulse of the song. Finally, children invent and adopt symbol systems to code rhythmic or pitch dimensions of the tune. In notation we see scribbles, images, words and abstract symbols used to capture the lyrics of the song, its structure, melodic contour and rhythmic grouping of the pitches.

Research suggests that children's invented notations fall into Bruner's representational types from recorded actions and distilled images to the emergence of symbolic language. Although the sequence from motion and image to the linguistic types of representation portrays how children naturally progress toward language in broad terms, the scope is not sufficiently articulated to include the development which continues with training. A more articulated model is necessary to explain the cracks in the working knowledge of older students. Skill theory provides just that level of detail.

Skill theory provides a more articulated means of tracing the details of musical development as it extends from physical co-ordinations to representations and, finally, to abstractions and principles. Accordingly three characteristic steps toward increasingly complex behaviours can be identified within each tier of development (Fischer 1980). Generally, this framework maps the geometrically expanding mental structures which occur with maturity and interaction with the environment across a range of increasingly complex tasks. The first step is a matter of regulating single dimensions of a task, the later steps involve co-ordinating simple relations between any two dimensions of a task, and finally, being able to systematically integrate complex interactions of relations within a task. Simply put, skill theory characterizes cognitive development as the skill of regulating or co-ordinating one, two, or two sets of two dimensions of a task within a domain.

Looking again at young children's music notations through skill theory, we can see a more differentiated and integrated cognitive theoretical description of the task of writing down a familiar song (Davidson and Scripp 1988a). Skill theory allows us to see the increasing control of dimensions independent of the type of representational system employed in the invented notations of young children.

Developmentally, early enactive notations of the 4 and 5 year old appear to be little more than tracks left by actions carried out with pen in hand, but actually they may record discrete events within a phrase through the movement of the hand, for example recording a *single dimension* of the task, the rhythmic pulse of the phrase. Gradually, children become able to represent more than one dimension of the phrase at a time. They may continue to make the same kind of enactive notation but now show both pulse and the grouping of the rhythmic structure of the phrase – thus mapping *two relational dimensions* of rhythm within the phrase.

Eventually, at the age of 7, more musically developed children begin to invent representations of *relations of systems* in their notations of the phrase. Using enactive, iconic or symbolic representations children simultaneously map two relational aspects of the rhythm along with mapping the contour of the pitches of the phrase. This creates a notation which co-ordinates the words of a song, indications of phrase structure, and its melodic and rhythmic shape (Fig. 4.1). We see yet more articulated evidence of cognitive development in music.

Impressive as this development is with untrained children, between the ages of 5 and 7, not until after a period of musical instruction do we expect to see successful attempts to construct a more fully dimensionalized notation which includes phrase structure, regular pulse and surface rhythm co-ordinated by metre, contour and pitches co-ordinated by a scale or key. Creating this level of notational representation demonstrates the ability to integrate complex interactions of systems or systems of skills.

While there is rapid development of notational systems in young children, there is little evidence that this growth continues without the support of musical training. Notations of simple songs by untrained 8 year olds look very much like those of 12 year olds, 16 year olds and 20 year olds. It appears that the advantage of experience with notation systems in other domains or much more exposure to songs does little to aid the adult attempting to make a music notation. The example in Figure 4.2 is typical of notations made by untrained adults.

Like the development of notation skills, the developmental sequence of early untrained musical production skills is equally impressive. We need only observe the young child's growing command of song-singing to appreciate the impressive span of development that appears from birth to about the age of 7.

Research strongly suggests that children construct their own understanding of the tonal materials of music (Davidson 1985). Rather than wholesale adaptation of model tunes or using certain intervallic units without tonal reference, the child constructs stable melodic structures, 'contour schemes', that are expanded and filled in with development. The complexity of children's repertoire of standard and invented songs expands predictably through a sequence of ordered levels of tonal vocabulary. In both cases –

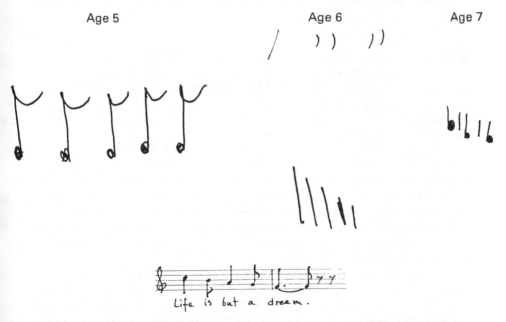

Figure 4.1   Developmental sequence of young children's notation of the final phrase of 'Row, Row, Row Your Boat' showing increasing control over dimensions in notation.
Age 5: Identifying the units of the phrase. Age 6: Notation showing the rhythmic grouping *or* the melodic contour. Age 7: Notation showing the rhythmic grouping *with* the melodic contour.

Figure 4.2   Notations of the first phrase of 'Happy Birthday' by musically untrained adults.

learnt and invented songs – development appears as largely self-constructed and increasingly sophisticated until, by the age of 7 or 8, children can invent or sing familiar songs with adult-like tonal stability, flexibility and nuance. Thus, by tracking the ability to learn unfamiliar tunes or generate original tunes, we see, at the age of 7 or 8, an integration of musical skills similar to that observed in notations.

The 2 year old begins to learn a song by initially focusing on the *single dimension* of words. The musical performance at this level remains largely undifferentiated with rhythm and melodic gestures rooted in speech. By the age of 4 or 5 the preschool child learns to produce the rhythmic surface of the song while independently using contour schemes to approximate the direction and scope of the melodic contour. At this level, children can handle more than one dimension of music, not only combining musical features such as rhythm and pitch but also beginning to extract dimensions from melodies such as the rhythmic surface or melodic pitches in isolation and without the support of the lyrics. Finally, the 7 year old begins to combine a sense of underlying pulse while projecting clear intervallically matched contours, as well as some expressive nuance (Davidson, McKernon and Gardner 1981). Also at this point, children begin to integrate contour schemes by making spontaneous use of the scale system of the culture – to co-ordinate the multiple systems necessary for song performance (Fig. 4.3).

As with notation skills, the developmental trajectory of song singing skills drops off around the age of 8, unless there is training. In many ways, simple

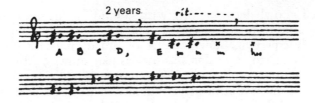

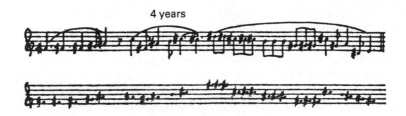

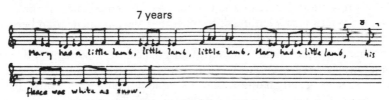

Figure 4.3   Stages of song learning in children aged 2 years, 4 years and 7 years.

songs sung by an adult musical novice may not differ a great deal from those of the normal 8 year old (Fig. 4.4).

We can view a range of musical development without the support or intervention of music lessons or classes. Looking at untrained children we can see the level of spontaneous and rehearsed singing (Davidson 1985; Davidson and Scripp 1988a; Dowling and Harwood 1986; McKernon 1979; Moorhead and Pond 1978; Werner 1961), the emergence of invented representations (Bamberger and Schon 1979; Bamberger 1986; Davidson and Scripp 1988a; Upitis 1985, 1987) and levels of compositions (Davidson and Welsh 1988; Scripp, Meyaard and Davidson 1988; Swanwick and Tillman 1986) all developing in various ways across adolescence into adulthood.

Summing up, spectacularly rapid changes in musical notations and performances of songs provide evidence of young children's increasingly

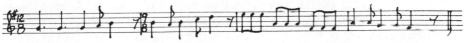

Figure 4.4   Performance of 'Row, Row, Row Your Boat' by a musically untrained adult.

sophisticated knowledge of music. With notation skills, not only are they increasingly able to focus on musical aspects of the tune, but we see the spontaneously emerging underpinnings of broad and deep literacy skills which reach across to other domains such as map drawing, storytelling and concepts of quantity (Wolf *et al.* 1988). Untrained children not only capture the structure of musical information but also invent ways of using familiar conventional and abstract symbols to suit the task. However, without specific musical training, adults do not improve significantly on the notations of children (Davidson, Scripp and Welsh, 1988).

When researchers attempt to go further to explain the cognitive underpinnings of notational development, they begin to face the interaction of development and formal musical training. For example, looking at the representation of isolated simple rhythms, researchers find evidence for two competing conceptions of musical events. In the simple rhythm 'one, two buckle my shoe' children may feature the *figural* (rhythmic groupings) or the more *formal* (metrical) aspects of the rhythm (Bamberger 1986; Upitis 1987). According to Upitis, musical novices tend to stay with a more figural description while musical training tends to support both figural and metrical features in the representations. Bamberger argues for the emergence of the figural–formal transaction as a hallmark for cognitive development (Bamberger and Schon 1979).

Another example of the interaction of musical development and training through musical representation is illustrated by asking children and adults to play familiar songs on an unfamiliar instrument (Bamberger 1986). Taking a set of physically identical bells (a Montessori set), Bamberger asked untrained and trained children to play and represent the song, 'Twinkle, Twinkle, Little Star'. In both their explorations and representations children exhibit two diverse types of knowledge: mapping the tune figurally and constructing the formal system, children find and represent the sequential order of pitches. Although the strategy records the path the melody takes, it reflects little of the structure of the tune or of the tonal system underlying the melody. A response more typical of her older or more trained subjects reveals a shift toward acknowledging redundancies in the pitches (or number) of bells required to play or represent the tune. With development, untrained adults (and children who have received additional training) become more interested in establishing the underlying musical scale to the tune, while recording the path of the melody as it is played on the bells.

From an educational perspective, these findings point to the role of musical training to support the development of musical representation skills. Matching curriculum to developmental levels, teaching the more 'figural' aspects of music may make more sense for the beginner. The time spent exploring the figural aspects of rhythmic grouping or pitch path may lead, later, to a smoother integration with the more formal aspects of notational system. For musicians, this may allow for an easier, more 'transactional' knowledge of musical dimensions.

Musically untrained children's song-singing gives another warning about early music education. For the child who sings with contour schemes, accommodating the concept of specific pitches of songs within the structure of scales may pre-empt the development of broad-based representational systems. Similarly, the child who cannot extract pulse from rhythm, may not appreciate or be able to use the concept of metre. A developmental view also carries implications for adults. For the adult with instrumental skills, it may be necessary to retrace this developmental sequence with the voice to begin co-ordinating instrumental skills with a similar set of skills expressed vocally (Davidson and Scripp 1988b).

Interaction of musical development and training

Returning to the laboratory imagined in our introduction and the examples of musical notations presented earlier, it is possible to witness puzzling aspects of musical development. The relationship of age and training may not provide uncontested examples of musical growth. Figure 4.5 provides a richly inventive notation of a nursery song by a child at age 7, while a preparatory student at a conservatory unsuccessfully tries to use standard notation to write down a song he could easily play from notation on his instrument. The first notation, for the psychologist, represents a crowning achievement of unfolding musical development while the second represents a disturbing reminder to the teacher that familiarity with conventional education and notation systems may not promote the necessary mastery of reliable literacy skills.

When making a notation, musically experienced adults bring much more information about what a music notation should capture to the task than untrained children and adults. For example, they assume the use of different graphic symbols to represent different musical dimensions: the staff, a clef and notes to show pitch, and a metre, measures and different durations to indicate rhythm. However, at the beginning of their professional training, it appears that many students know more *about* musical symbols than they can *use* successfully (as in Fig. 4.5). As in our example, some students unknowingly shift their focus from rhythm to pitch relations during the task. When challenged, many make the assumption that all the dimensions they attempted to notate are accurately reflected in their notation, although they are unable to co-ordinate their knowledge of the two dimensions. In Bruner's terms, they approach the task using the more sophisticated symbolic representations, but in terms of skill theory, these notations represent only an intermediate step toward the full co-ordination of rhythmic and pitch dimensions.

In their case the young child invents a symbol system that captures some of the melodic, lyrical and rhythmic aspects of a melody. When reading back the notation, the symbols work to remind her of the features important to her performance. The conservatory student, on the other hand, employs standard notation but no longer controls the integration of sight and sound. Claiming the tune was written correctly he sings back the tune he knows, but *not* the

Figure 4.5 Two notations of 'Row, Row, Row Your Boat' made by a 7 year old and a 16 year old music student.

melody he would hear if he played it back on his instrument. Where the child maps according to his or her level of musical understanding, the music student fails to integrate performance, perception and musical concepts with the task.

In the domain of performance we observe the relationship of two skills essential to musical development: learning to read music while playing an instrument. Imagine the beginning guitar student (age 8) playing for the first time in front of an audience. From his perspective the performance is going well. He plays confidently with a feeling that all the notes were played at the right place on the fingerboard and was pleased to get through it all 'without a hitch'. Unfortunately for the audience, he had tuned the strings of his guitar incorrectly and scarcely anyone recognized the tune 'Down in the Valley'. Another guitar student – an advanced student at New England Conservatory – was studying her literature in another way. Not content to rehearse the fingers alone, she was singing her part – and other accompanying parts – from the score. What was hard to realize in one modality was explored in another. Her voice and fingers were working interactively toward an original interpretation of the composition.

Both of these examples show the rich interplay of musical thinking with developing musical skills. In the case of performance knowledge, the beginning guitarist sees only the necessity of linking finger action with the instrument. The sound of the music appears to exist independently of this kinaesthetic co-ordination of finger and tablature. For the more advanced guitarist it is necessary to do more than perform with the instrument. Music reading must also integrate knowledge of the accompanying texture with the melodic line – all through the voice and the internalized tonal systems represented in the score.

Developmentally, early enactive representations of music may appear to be little more than action patterns carried out on the instrument, modelling a single dimension of the task, the ability to produce a pitch on demand. Gradually, children become able to represent enactively more than one dimension of the music at a time. They may appear to continue to make the same kind of action patterns as before, but now these may also show some aspect of rhythm, the pulse or the grouping of the rhythmic structure of the phrase. At this level, the child is mapping two relational dimensions of pitch (and rhythm).

Eventually more musically developed children begin to represent relations of systems in their performance of a phrase. Using enactive representations, the player simultaneously performs two relational aspects, the pitch and the rhythm – knitting the individual notes into the contour of the phrase while regulating the rhythmic durations with the underlying pulse. Ultimately, this creates a performance which conveys the pitches as an expressive melodic shape because they are joined by articulations, dynamic shaping, and rhythmic nuance.

Not until after an extended period of musical training do we expect to see attempts to construct a fully dimensionalized performance complete with phrase structure, surface rhythm and a pulse co-ordinated by metre, as well as pitches integrated into melodic contours, themselves co-ordinated by a scale, and expressed by sensitive control of temporal and tonal nuance. According to skill theory, to be able to create this level of enactive representation demonstrates the ability to integrate complex interactions or systems of skills.

What about creative expression and musical development? One question not addressed in the developmental research so far is the growth of creative expression. How might skill growth and the underlying cognitive structures be traced in more traditionally creative applications of musical expression? Traditionally only seen with training, several lines of research have explored composing with untrained subjects as well.

If a relation between cognitive growth and creative expression exists, we would expect the compositions of untrained children to show a similar developmental track to that observed in notation and performance. In an important developmental study of music composition, the transcription of children's improvisations documents the shifts which lead from self-absorbed exploration of materials through improvisation to reflection on materials used in self-aware solutions of self-imposed problems in music expression (Swanwick and Tillman 1986).

Reflecting the work of Piaget, Swanwick's reflects the child's initial grasp of musical materials and the later mastery of them. This direction of growth also reflects the child's increasing ability to decentre from self.

Four broad, two-step levels characterize children's musical development from age 3 to 15: sensory manipulation, imitation, imaginative play and reflection. Each of the levels is begun in self-absorbed exploration and ends with self-aware solutions of self-posed musical problems. At the first level, the child concentrates on the mastery of materials. The child uses composition as a vehicle for exploring the sensory-motor aspects of playing and of manipulating notes and rhythms with relatively little attention to expressiveness. During the second level, the child makes pieces which are expressive and borrow from materials from the vernacular. During the third level, the child's engagement in imaginative play leads to playing with (and developing a sensitivity to) musical form. As the child becomes aware of the position of his or her work within a tradition, and of music's expressive impact, he begins to reflect on his own thought processes and those of others. This final stage of development, Swanwick proposes, is represented by a focus on musical values.

A spiral of assimilation and accommodation exists within each of these levels, mapping children's developmental shift from an absorption with their own individual work to an appreciation of tradition and the social aspects of their work. Thus this growth reflects the child's increasing ability to decentre from self. Furthermore, the movement within the assimilation–accommodation scaffolding parallels the child's initial grasp of musical materials and later mastery of them.

This research suggests intriguing connections between stages of musical conception through inventing music. Increasingly, with or without training, it appears musicians seek a greater sophistication of musical conception directed at first with more skilful manipulation of musical materials, later grasping the vernacular and idiom of the culture, and finally the construction of free-standing compositional systems that express individual criteria of musical values. Opposed to vocal performance and notational skills, there is as yet little evidence that untrained musicians can engage in formal compositional problem-solving using standard notation.

However, in our laboratory there is a new addition: the computer. Today we see teachers and researchers using computers in ways that extend the boundaries of musical development, particularly with regard to composition. Using powerful 'user-friendly' composing software (e.g. Deluxe Music Construction Set 1986, on Macintosh), untrained children and adults can engage in composition tasks that suggest very strongly that musical development continues in spite of a lack of training in musical notation, performance or ear training – let alone composition lessons! Observing trained children and adults also suggests that the computer as a composing aid also helps music students, especially as they approach more difficult tasks.

Computer support provides another clear look at all four cells in our research approach. For example, the full range of subjects, with a minimum of instruction with the computer, were able to provide a harmony part to the tune 'Twinkle, Twinkle, Little Star'. Comparing untrained children with adults suggests that children, despite more experience and enthusiasm for the computer, fail to perform as well as adult novices (Scripp, Meyaard and Davidson 1988). Children between the ages of 8 and 13 were simply less apt to create musical cadences, resolve dissonances or create singable independent duet lines than adults. Indeed, with this simple harmonization problem, untrained adults performed on a par with conservatory students when given the scaffolding provided by the computer (Fig. 4.6).

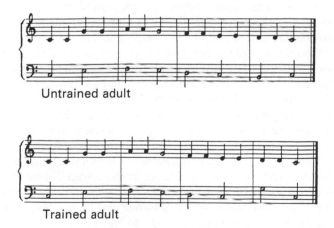

Untrained adult

Trained adult

Figure 4.6   Two solutions to a simple composition task by musically untrained and trained adults.

Although untrained adults and children both agreed on what constituted good solutions to the task (by choosing their favourite or best duet lines from a small library of examples), only the adult novices were able to construct musical solutions along the lines of their perceptual preferences. This research shows how the computer supports the integration of musical production (compositional choices), perception (monitoring computer playback), coded and revised in standard notation (manipulating symbols to represent musical computations).

How does the computer assist the trained musician? Although the products of adult novices and conservatory undergraduates were virtually indistinguishable, the composing process differed greatly. While the novice spends an enormous amount of time experimenting, listening to playback and revising time and time again, the conservatory student often ignores the playback and edit features of the computer, using it only to enter notes. It appears that the more expert subjects spend less time monitoring the results mechanically. A literate musician is able to internalize the operations of the symbol system, thus making it possible to hear the notational representation of musical ideas internally. Therefore it is not surprising that advanced conservatory students consistently report solving this duet line with the inner ear. With such a simple task, the conservatory student made relatively little use of the computer beyond recording the solution on the 'note processor'.

When the task demanded more musical sophistication, however, the use of the computer support becomes critical in different ways to both the adult novice and conservatory student. In the example below, added accidentals to the duet part imply a new type of solution. Due to lack of familiarity with musical norms, the musical novice interprets the new notes initially as wrong notes. The conservatory sophomore, however, digs into the now more interesting problem. Since simple responses no longer can be applied, relatively unfamiliar solutions need to be discovered and may even require a new working process. The conservatory student now experiments and revises extensively, using the computer playback more often in the process, much like the novice did on the simple 'Twinkle' task (Fig. 4.7).

In this example, we see the computer as a new arena for observing musical development in terms of the interaction of cognitive skill growth and training. For untrained children between the ages of 8 and 13, the computer does little to enhance composing. This is in spite of the availability of standard notation and performance playback provided by the software. For adult novices, the computer offers new 'zones of proximal development' for composing skills. The support structure of the computer allows us to specify task conditions in ways which enable us to observe trained and untrained responses to problem-solving. Novices can now problem-solve in the context of the conventional symbol system, monitoring results without the prerequisite of a performance instrument. With 'optimal support' (Fischer and Pipp 1984), adult novices react in surprisingly sophisticated ways to modelled solutions of compositional problems, working up new solutions to more advanced musical problems (Scripp, Meyaard and Davidson 1988).

Untrained adult

Trained adult

Figure 4.7 Two solutions to a more complex composition task by musically un-trained and trained adults.

For the educator, the computer offers an intriguing substitute for the support provided by conventional musical training. The integration of no-tational, problem-solving and performance skills – 'simulated' by using the computer – represents a new approach to musical literacy and provides the skills necessary for the operationalization of the complex and highly differ-entiated musical dimensions necessary for problem-solving in musical com-position. Supported by technology and the helping hands of teachers we can finally see a richer portrait of musical development.

Music education: the emergence of reflective knowledge through literacy skills

In this section we enter the top floors of our laboratory, where the highest levels of skill and artistry are the goals and centres of activity. We will attempt to portray the highest levels of musical development from the view of literacy skills. Literacy skills imply a working integration of musical knowledge. Not limited to the learning of conventional codes for nomenclature, isolated music symbols or fluency in instrumental techniques, literacy skills form the capstone of musical development. Going beyond repetitive training of musi-cal facts, historical anecdotes or fingering of passages toward the internal-ization and integration of musical performance skills with representational, compositional or conceptual knowledge, literacy skills represent the fullest and richest knowledge of musical performance, reflection and perception. Fully operationalized literacy skills are often strikingly clear in the best of conductors, who for example, need to discriminate unintentional deviations from the score from interpretative ideas. These skills make it possible to go beyond the information provided by the composer, and freely demonstrate internalized musical ideas without the use of an instrument. In terms of skill theory outlined above, musicians who develop considerable literacy skills are functioning at the level of complex abstractions (integrating tonality, thematic development, recursive implications of phrasing, etc.) and constructing sensory-motor descriptions of (or solutions to) musical problems of interpretation.

What promotes musical literacy? Rarely do literacy skills naturally unfold without extensive training. Professional levels of these skills require an intensive programme of special support. However, the support must be broad-based. There is little certainty that these literacy skills develop even with intensive individualized instrumental instruction and knowledge of musical repertoire. Understanding the difference between the development of broad literacy skills and specialized musical training is crucial to our discussion of the upper levels of musical development.

For example, does instrumental training (from ages 6 to 18) predict the development of literacy skills? From the maturational view, literacy skills are acquired only as needed. From the cultural transmission point of view, these years provide considerable time for the serious music student to be exposed to and assimilate the principles of music notation, standards of musical performance and a range of musical literature. For the cognitive-developmentalist, a range of problems that demand the integration of performance, perception and representational skills is necessary to stimulate and guide the development of music literacy skill.

In the 'Happy Birthday' experiment mentioned previously, the continued lack of integrated literacy skills after many years of instrumental lessons is all too clear (Davidson, Scripp and Welsh 1988). Asking entering students at a major conservatory to write down the all too familiar tune 'Happy Birthday' without the use of their instrument produces sobering results. Surprising to most music educators (let alone educators outside of music), a majority of students entering professional training are unable to write down the tune with complete accuracy. More striking, students blithely 'read' incorrect notations back, singing the correct tune while ignoring the difference between what they sing and what they have written. That is, they are unable to take advantage of every opportunity to discriminate between the score and the performance. These results indicate the important difference and severe disparity between vocal performance of the song, knowledge of an instrument and its repertoire, and knowledge of the symbol system which carries information from composer to performer.

In the face of a severe lack of integration of musical perception and representation, performance becomes entirely dependent on memory – whether in the fingers, in the ear or in verbal description. Repertoire acquisition on the instrument becomes the only model of musical knowledge. Displaying a lack of internalization, musical development fails to include a range of integrated knowledge. The remembered sound of known tunes or normal notational images do not match. Without their instruments, students are unable to relate their image of the song to its notated form. Handed their instruments, however, students quickly realize their notational errors and can revise them accordingly. Typically, however, a lack of co-ordination among musical skills fails to inform a more actively constructed sense of music imagery, memorized or not.

Is this fragmentation of musical skills inevitable? Analysis of typical errors of conservatory students suggests that when literacy skills are not developed alongside technical instrumental training, the result is a fragmented knowledge of music and ultimate disintegration of skills. When literacy skills fail to develop, students compensate for the lack of integration in their training by substituting 'what they know about music' for what they hear. For example, we continually see the error characteristic of this group: assuming that all simple melodies begin and end on the same note (assumed to be the tonic). In our study, a common error type reflects the distortion produced by this concept. The last phrase of 'Happy Birthday' was represented as ending on the note with which the song begins regardless of the function of the opening note.

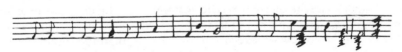

Figure 4.8   Notations of 'Happy Birthday' by entering conservatory students, showing typical confusion about ending of last phrase.

We see different results in an environment of musical training which links growth in performance, representation and composition. These solutions to musical problems are more characteristic of our cognitive-developmental model of musical growth. For example, adolescents who receive extensive ear training, theory and composition do much better with the notation task. They are able to express the metre, compare phrases of the melody within the key structure of the tune and make revisions or refinements after performing the tune 'in their head'. Errors for these students are a matter of refining perceptual knowledge rather than substituting ungrounded musical concepts (Davidson, Scripp and Welsh 1988).

The adolescents, who were able to best co-ordinate their knowledge of the tune 'Happy Birthday', typically had some experience with other modes of musical knowledge. These students had additional experience with counterpoint, composition and solfège (the skill of singing at sight with identifying pitch names). Anything but remedial in nature, these basic skill courses provide a novel opportunity to reintegrate musical skills to keep pace with repertoire knowledge and general musical development. Even for the more mature musician, these courses provide a special opportunity to extend skill across multiple representations of musical expression and thought. Examples of the extent of musical literacy skills include perception (error detection), performance across multiple modalities (implying a correlation between instrumental and vocal sight reading skills), representation (dictation or transcription skills) and composing (improvisational skills in keyboard harmony). The multiple manifestations of sight-singing skills expand to become a 'clearing house' for later expression and testing of musical concepts.

Judging instrumental performance in terms of accuracy alone devalues interpretative or expressive development central to conservatory training. Developmental studies of sight-singing pose an interesting alternative view: assessing literacy skills qualitatively through error analysis rather than quantitatively in terms of error count (Davidson, Scripp and Meyaard 1988). Stressing such cognitively higher-order skills as the ability to recover from mistakes, resist false inference or support, or select melodic passages from a full score all suggest a different kind of development which extends beyond simple mirroring of instrumental literature with the voice.

Protocol analysis of in-class performance suggests developmental levels that can be described by qualitative measures. We see students grappling first with simple melodies in one key or rhythmic subdivision and later with melodies that modulate. Developmental frameworks essentially define levels of complexity where errors record instances of difficulty, misunderstanding or abandonment, and are indicative of levels of strategies and approaches leading to stability of execution in various manifestations of problem-solving.

Another example comes from research in problem-solving – this time from composition. Asking beginning and advanced conservatory students to compose a modulating melody (based on the rhythm of a Schubert melody) reveals very different levels on the 'developmental path' of composing strategies (Davidson and Welsh 1988). In the early undergraduate years, the representation of the problem, the working styles, and the strategies employed, all suggest radically different states of musical knowledge from those of the more advanced student. Through two levels of tonal thinking – the enactive and the reflective – we see students progressing from small working units on the piano to conceiving and internalizing solutions at the length of the phrase.

This example once again shows the power and the limitation of our general developmental model in music education. Whether it is untrained children's first invented notations or college music students composing short melodies, musical knowledge appears to proceed from the local enactive explorations to the more symbolic, systematic and reflective command of musical thinking. However, the rate of musical development in representation and production can differ greatly. As with notation, development of instrumental repertoire and the ability to write tonally convincing melodies differ greatly. Rather than being age-specific, an element of interaction with musical training is necessary before levels can be reasonably aligned across tasks or modalities of expression. Formal musical systems and knowledge of musical norms can stimulate students to construct their own sense of reference and stability across a range of problems that may beg for multiple solutions (such as the composing task, or selecting melodic lines to sing from a full score).

Similar to the 'natural' developmental sequences, training catalyses new levels of musical thinking into increasingly complex skills. In a cognitive-developmental approach, as development trails off, training begins to lead. When appropriate levels of task complexity are introduced, an individual's problem-solving skills are engaged and cognitive restructuring occurs. Cognitive psychologists refer to the more advanced levels in terms of reflective thinking. The reflective musician is more apt to demonstrate declarative knowledge (concepts that stand for events, strings of events or abstractions) or procedural knowledge (analysis or descriptions about how things are accomplished). These form the basis for reflective thinking about music.

This later period of musical development with training marks a 'cognitive shift' as formidable as the 7 to 9 year old shift with untrained children. The shift to a more reflective description of musical thought represents a cognitive restructuring of musical actions, perceptions and understandings that supports more powerfully integrated musical skills. However, the early phase of this level of development may feature a state of instability, as various forms of musical representations compete for descriptions of musical knowing.

For the young musician in a small ensemble, rehearsing and coaching may involve systems of representations that offer multiple descriptions of what formerly could be expressed in single concepts. Intonation, for example, can be a matter of kinesthetic technique (bowing, fingering, embouchure), an aural discrimination or independent internalized image mapped to physical technique, or a systematically integrated concept related to particular tonal, stylistic or historical context. As more formal and sophisticated representations of musical events or processes gain currency in musical interactions, young performers restructure their musical thinking. Correcting intonation may not be facilitated by telling young children they are playing too high when their understanding of pitch may only be linked with embouchure pressure or the needle of a tuning machine. Asking them to sing their part may more effectively reveal the level of development of self-constructed concept of intonation. On the other hand, teaching violin students about baroque tuning or the effect of harmonic context without sufficient motor skills to produce conventional temperaments may also prove counter-productive.

In sum, reflective thinking, from a cognitive-developmental perspective, develops with the interaction of motor skills and literacy skills that enable the student to link performance, concept and percept. Reflective thinking appears as an important dimension of musical development that arises from the more enactive stages where skills are first manifest, and are later linked to the symbolic literacy skills of the musical culture. The most effective levels of a musical education must encompass this perspective.

Musical pedagogies as perspectives on cognitive development

During this century, two influential approaches in American music education of children were originally formulated in response to problems in professional schools of music. Each represents penetrating and insightful reflections on musical development. The problems they address show up in the professional schools, but the solutions to those problems lie in the earliest years of musical training.

Shinichi Suzuki (1969) and Emile Jaques-Dalcroze (1912, 1921) observe that students at professional music schools do not always demonstrate mastery over a wide range of musical skills. However, their complaints and solutions to problems in higher levels of training point to very different orientations of early musical development. Acknowledging their contribution to musical education, we will now look at these pedagogies and determine the 'goodness of fit' with our cognitive-developmental framework.

In the Suzuki class performance we see rows of children standing with small violins, all playing the same melodic line from a series of progressively harder pieces. No music stands are necessary. The performance displays young children's remarkable power to learn many pieces by memory. With more difficult pieces, fewer children participate in the performance. With the final piece of the programme only the few, most experienced students are playing.

In the Dalcroze classroom a very different story unfolds. At first children move all around the room, exploring the space while listening to improvised music on the piano. Trained in special movements and solfège syllables, children respond to the music by mapping the pulse, register, pitches or form of the music with their bodies and voices. Finally, children are encouraged to improvise on their own, creating short musical fragments that the others can respond to.

The first approach, Suzuki violin training, centres on acquiring musical knowledge through instrumental skill. Beginning the study of the violin as an adult, and disillusioned with conservatory education in Japan (Ueno Academy), Suzuki studied theory, acoustics and the violin with private teachers in Japan and Germany. Perhaps as a result of his own frustration while learning the violin as an adult Suzuki turned his attention to the education of very young children. Today his methods have been adopted world-wide with great success.

Of particular interest is the psychological orientation implicit in his training. Stressing the metaphor of the language acquisition in a highly supportive environment, Suzuki believes that 'any child is able to display highly superior abilities only if the correct methods are used in training'. Talent is not considered inherited but rather a product of the child's adaptation to the environment. However, it is not clear how much musical development can take place without 'optimal conditions'. Suzuki often speaks of the development of talent as entirely dependent on the quality of particular environmental conditions: 'It is a frightening fact. By no means only words or music, but everything, good or bad, is absorbed' (Suzuki 1969: 17); 'What does not exist in the environment is not developed' (p. 23).

For Suzuki, the quality of environment alone determines the level of musical skills likely to develop. Using the example of how nightingales learn from 'master teachers':

Whether the wild bird will develop good or bad singing quality is indeed decided in the first month by the voice and tone of its teacher . . . If it has a good teacher, the infant bird will, through physiological transformation, learn from experience to produce tones as beautiful as those of its teacher. But, if an infant bird is brought to such a teacher after being raised by wild nightingales, there is always failure, as long experience has shown.

(Suzuki 1969: 19)

Accordingly, learning occurs through the accumulation of new skills that can be used to replace old habits. This method of learning may extend across types of musical knowledge. Using poor solfège singing as an example, Suzuki offers strictly quantified perceptual habituation as a solution:

If they have learned the wrong 'fa' (fourth degree of the scale) by hearing it five thousand times, one must make them listen to the right 'fa' six thousand or seven thousand times . . . when the number reaches five and six thousand times, the ability to produce the correct 'fa' acquired by listening to it six thousand times begins to take precedence over the ability to produce the wrong 'fa' that was acquired by listening only five thousand times.

(Suzuki 1969: 101–2)

Here the emphasis on repetitive, rote learning is clear. The first stages of instruction involve listening to carefully prepared tapes of Suzuki literature. At first through perception and later through the fingers, the student develops performance skills. Through the psychological and physiological accommodation to the violin comes the musical acculturalization. Although a tremendous repertoire can be acquired through this method, interactions with perception, representation and composition outside the instrument are not particularly encouraged. Only at some later time, for example, will the child develop literacy skills sufficient for participating in ensemble playing with music.

The second approach is in stark contrast to the first. Dalcroze warns against early specialization of musical training on any instrument. Instead, Dalcroze training begins by preparing the child for the repertoire learning that occurs later on the instrument. If the musical mind is the aim of education, instrumental technique may initially impede such development. Complaining about the premature specialization of instrumental skills, Dalcroze warns that 'playing in the present day has specialized in a finger technique which takes no account of the faculty of mental expression. It is no longer a means, it has become an end' (Dalcroze 1912: 16).

In direct contrast to Suzuki, Dalcroze would have the child improvise music before engaging in repertoire learning by imitation.

> Improvisation is the study of the direct relationship between cerebral commands and muscular interpretations in order to express one's own musical feelings. Performance is propelled by developing the students' power of sensation, imagination, and memory. It is not based on direct imitation of the teacher's performance.
>
> (Dalcroze 1932: 371)

Following a sequence of activities from bodily expression of rhythmics, to the operationalization of pitch and rhythms represented through solfège syllables, and finally to improvisation the young musician is being trained in early literacy skills before the acquisition of repertoire is begun.

The orientation of this pedagogical approach is, again, in stark contrast to learning Suzuki violin. The Dalcroze child's musical development depends more on how the child approaches and experiences music than how the young child adapts to repertoire or technical models that imitate cultural norms. From the Brunerian view discussed earlier, the child first learns to express musical properties through the body, enactively. This is not unlike the orientation of Suzuki. With Suzuki, notation is learnt after the child can play many pieces on the violin, whereas with Dalcroze, the child constructs intermediary representations that will later guide the instrument.

These two methods of music education also measure musical development in contrasting ways. Where the Suzuki violinist learns to memorize and play through a continuum of progressively more difficult pieces, the Dalcroze child learns to play the instrument only after command of musical language has been demonstrated through improvisation – skills that not only encapsulate theoretical concepts about music but also allow the child to reconstruct and combine this knowledge into new musical expressions.

Summing up, we see ideas about musical development through the lens of successful pedagogies. Both methods show a concern for the early stages of music learning and stress the physical, enactive mode of representation of music, standards of musicianship *co-ordinated* with the use of standard notation systems. However, neither of these examples were based on developmental psychological models as much as practical teaching methods designed after close observation. Although both models are extremely effective, they represent two contrasting approaches to music instruction: the cultural transmission, associative-learning model and the progressive, cognitive-developmental model.

Their psychological orientation differs in several ways. Development in one is continual, progressive and learnt through externalized imitation and rote repetition. Suzuki violinists support the shared experience of learning a particular sequence of pieces from the literature, repeated continually throughout the years of training. In the Dalcroze classroom, development initially features an unfolding of musical expression through a repertoire of physical motions and gestures (eurhythmics), then musical literacy skills through reading, writing and singing and, finally, personal experiments with improvisation at the piano. Dalcroze-trained children begin their instrumental studies with considerable and broad musical training already in place.

Formulating a cognitive-developmental model of music education

So far in this chapter we have argued for a cognitive-developmental view of music education and research. We would be remiss if we could not offer refinements in critiquing current pedagogical practice based on this view. Based on our analysis of two highly contrasted pedagogical approaches, we offer several criteria for more comprehensive pedagogical alternatives. Does the pedagogy feature:

- multiple representations of musical knowledge?
- ordered dimensions of modes of musical expression?
- tasks sequenced in order of complexity?
- age-related aspects of the pedagogical sequence?

Although Suzuki violin lessons are exciting, active experiences for the young child, the musical experience is primarily limited to expression with the instrument; Dalcroze offers ordered multiple representations of the music from the enactive to the representational. The musical dimensions are approached carefully in terms of the technique of the instrument (open strings first, repeated bowings) with Suzuki lessons; in Dalcroze classes the tasks are ordered by musical dimension (rhythm then pitch) with no particular acknowledgment of difficulty. While Suzuki repertoire is carefully sequenced, Dalcroze materials are uncertain. With teachers freely choosing and inventing music and students improvising, control of the levels of complexity is loose. Although both methods can be initiated at a very young age (2 to 4) there are few formal constraints in terms of age-specific tasks.

In the final analysis, we ask how any pedagogy fits into the developmental frameworks offered by cognitive psychology. Arguing for a music education which features the development of musical understanding as well as for the success of musical performance, we argue for mapping the two together. In a music environment where most children cannot afford intensive instruction, we need a model for musical education that effectively energizes the child in all manifestations of our musical culture.

Keeping musical productivity in the foreground, we see a musical education that features active music-making as the medium for musical development. The concept of musical production can be expanded to include compositional and representational aspects. Children need opportunity to express themselves musically in whatever mode they want. With scaled-down Suzuki violins, body gestures or computer-supported composing we can support a wider range of musical development in our schools. Music production involves children taking an active role. From this point of view musical perception should be linked with productivity and reflective thought. Discrimination or recognition skills linked with musical performance or composition ensures involvement in the whole process of music production. Reflective thinking informed by performance skills and linked to perception allows the whole musical experience to extend into the important social interaction and intrapersonal development that music can richly provide.

Conclusion

Looking at musical development in the music classroom and rehearsal is a difficult and daunting task, for the researcher and teacher alike. Music is a particularly rich domain where the motor or sensory co-ordinations must continue to inform and grow with the more abstract concepts necessary for musical literacy. Psychological frameworks of Bruner and Fischer help describe the intricacies of musical cognitive development and shed light on its path. Viewed from a psychological perspective, the symbol system is visible as the co-ordination of motor activities and reflective thinking in notation and performance. The symbol system becomes the transactional medium for physical co-ordination and musical ideas: from the notation to the finger-board. Swanwick's developmental framework for composition based on a spiralling progression of play and imitation describes the acquisition of cultural norms of musical expression through improvisation. With the computer, compositional development co-ordinated with standard notation can be observed and supported in music research and instruction.

Finally, advocates for educational reform bear the responsibility of incorporating the psychological frameworks that apply to musical development. The work of Bamberger, Upitis, Swanwick and other psychologists working in music directly bridge the gap between cognitive psychologists and music education. Critiques of long-standing pedagogies can be constructively employed through this approach. We need examples of ongoing collaboration between researchers and practitioners that integrate a developmental perspective with the demands of day-to-day instruction in schools. Successful future music education will look toward an era of music education informed by basic and applied research that extends beyond one-dimensional training and links musical skills in production, perception and reflection to our ongoing musical culture.

Acknowledgements

We gratefully acknowledge support from the following foundations: the Spencer Foundation for their funding of the Early Symbolizations Project, which yielded new findings about the emergence of children's songs; the Carnegie Foundation for their support of preschool and primary school children's music notations; the Markle Foundation for their support of learning and technology which allowed us to study musical composition with and without musical training; and the Rockefeller Foundation which is currently supporting research in assessment of music learning and development in middle and secondary schools. Finally, we wish to thank our Project Zero colleagues – Howard Gardner, David Perkins, Dennie Wolf, Joe Walters, Joan Meyaard and Martha Davis for their contributions and suggestions relating to our musical research.

References

Bamberger, J. (1986). 'Cognitive issues in the development of musically gifted children', in R. Sternberg and J. Davidson (eds.), *Conceptions of Giftedness*. Cambridge, Cambridge University Press.

Bamberger, J. and Schon, D. A. (1979). 'The figural-formal transaction'. Unpublished manuscript, MIT, Division for Study and Research in Education.

Blum, D. (1986). *The Art of Quartet Playing: The Guarneri Quartet in Conversation with David Blum*. New York, Knopf.

Bruner, J. (1973). 'The growth of representational processes in childhood', in J. Anlin (ed.), *Beyond the Information Given: Studies in the Psychology of Knowing*. New York, W. W. Norton.

Dalcroze, E. (1912). *The Eurythmics of Jaques-Dalcroze*. London, Constable & Co.

(1921). *Rhythm, Music and Education*. London, Putnam's Sons.

(1932). 'Rhythmic and pianoforte improvisation'. *Music and Letters*, 13(4): 371–80.

Davidson, L. (1985). 'Tonal structures of children's early songs'. *Music Perception*, 2(3): 361–74.

Davidson, L., McKernon, P. and Gardner, H. (1981). 'The acquisition of song: a developmental approach', in J. A. Mason *et al.* (eds.), *Documentary Report of the Ann Arbor Symposium*, Music Educators National Conference, Reston, Virginia.

Davidson, L. and Scripp, L. (1988a). 'Young children's musical representations: windows on music cognition', in J. Sloboda (ed.), *Generative Processes in Music*. Oxford, Clarendon Press.

(1988b). 'A developmental view of sightsinging'. *Journal of Music Theory Pedagogy*, 2(1), 10–23.

Davidson, L., Scripp, L. and Meyaard, J. (1988). 'Sightsinging ability: a quantitative and qualitative point of view'. *Journal of Music Theory Pedagogy*, 2(1): 51–68.

Davidson, L., Scripp, L. and Welsh, P. (1988). '"Happy Birthday": evidence for conflicts of perceptual knowledge and conceptual understanding'. *Journal of Aesthetic Education*, 22(1): 65–74.

Davidson, L. and Welsh, P. (1988). 'From collections to structure: the developmental path of tonal thinking', in J. Sloboda (ed.), *Generative Processes in Music.* Oxford, Clarendon Press.

Deluxe Music Construction Set (1986). Menlo Park, Calif, California Electronic Arts.

Dowling, W. J. and Harwood, D. L. (1986). *Music Cognition.* Orlando, Fla, Academic Press.

Feldman, D. H. (1986). 'How development works, in I. Levin (ed.), *Stage and Structure.* Norwood, NJ, Ablex.

Fischer, K. (1980). 'A theory of cognitive development: the control and construction of hierarchies of skills' *Psychological Review,* 87(6): 477–531.

Fischer, K. and Pipp, S. (1984). 'Processes of cognitive development: optimal level and skill acquisition', in R. J. Sternberg (ed.), *Mechanisms of Cognitive Development.* New York, W. H. Freeman & Co.

Kohlberg, L. and Mayer, R. (1972). 'Development as the aim of education'. *Harvard Educational Review,* 42(4): 449–96.

McKernon, P. E. (1979). 'The development of first songs in young children', in H. Gardner and D. Wolf (eds.), *Early Symbolisation.* San Francisco, Jossey-Bass.

Moorhead, G. E. and Pond, D. (1978). *Music of Young Children.* Santa Barbara, Calif., Pillsbury Foundation, 1941–51.

Piaget, J. (1962). *Play, Dreams and Imitation in Childhood.* New York, W. W. Norton.

— (1983). 'Piaget's theory', in P. H. Mussen (ed.), *Handbook of Child Psychology* (4th edn), vol. 1, ed. W. Kessen. New York, John Wiley.

Schon, D. A. (1987). *Educating the Reflective Practitioner.* San Francisco, Jossey-Bass.

Scripp, L. and Davidson, L. (1988). 'Framing the dimensions of sightsinging: teaching toward musical development'. *Journal of Music Theory Pedagogy,* 2(1): 24–50.

Scripp, L., Meyaard. J. and Davidson L. (1988). 'Discerning musical development: using computers to discover what we know'. *Journal of Aesthetic Education,* 22(1): 75–88.

Suzuki, S. (1969). *Nurtured by Love.* New York, Exposition Press.

Swanwick, K. and Tillman, J. (1986). 'The sequence of musical development: a study of children's composition'. *British Journal of Music Education,* 3(3): 305–39.

Upitis, R. (1985). 'Children's understanding of rhythm: the relationship between development and musical training'. Unpublished doctoral dissertation, Harvard University, Cambridge, Mass.

— (1987). 'Toward a model for rhythm development', in J. C. Peery, I. W. Peery, and T. W. Draper (eds.) *Music and Child Development.* New York, Springer-Verlag.

Vygotsky, L. (1978). *Mind in Society: The Development of Higher Psychological Processes.* Cambridge, Mass., Harvard University Press.

Werner, H. (1961). *Comparative Psychology of Mental Development.* New York, Science Editions.

Wolf, D., Davidson, L., Davis, M., Walters, J., Hodges, M. and Scripp, L. (1988). 'Beyond A, B, and C: a broader and deeper view of literacy', in A. D. Pellegrini (ed.), *Psychological Bases for Early Education.* New York, John Wiley.

5
Children as writers

Helen Cowie

From a very early age all of us engage in 'storying', creating fictions in which we replay and recombine actual experiences and construct imaginary extensions and alternatives to them.

(Wells 1985: 252)

Introduction

The present chapter is about children as story-writers. I have chosen to focus on stories since the narrative mode is one in which children spontaneously engage from a very early age. Sutton-Smith, for example, proposes that 'the mind is, amongst other things, a narrative concern. Dreams are universal and so are stories' (Sutton-Smith 1988: 22). Bruner and Haste describe the characteristic cultural dramas which underline 'the possible roles, actions and self-definitions' (Bruner and Haste 1987: 89) open to the individual in a social context, and suggest that 'sensitivity to narrative provides the major link between our own sense of self and our sense of others in the social world around us' (p. 94). Children create stories not only to make sense of an experience but also to explore alternative ways of enacting that experience.

In order to understand the writing process, we must look at the abilities which the young child brings to the task of communicating in writing, so I start by considering the importance of the child's experience of telling stories, of creating narrative sequences in play and of describing people and events through the medium of drawing. I also examine the development of the child's concept of story with particular focus on the growth of a sense of narrative structure. I look next at the ways in which children use narrative writing to become more socially aware, to develop greater sensitivity to the needs of others, to experiment with social roles and to explore events in the world of the imagination; and present children's accounts of their own experiences as story-writers. Finally, I discuss the role of parents and teachers in facilitating the writing process.

Early stages in writing development

Long before they write, many children seem to have developed hypotheses about what writing is and how it may be used. Children often show an interest in the use of marks as a mode of expression (Clay 1975; Ferreiro and Teberesky 1982) and integrate their playful interest in 'storying' with their capacity to create figures and shapes on paper. Vygotsky saw the scribbles which preschool children produce as 'the first precursors of future writing' (Vygotsky 1978: 115). Gardner (1980) has observed that as early as the age of 2, some children have categorized certain activities as 'writing' and will try to imitate the flow of a script. Often these marks, which may appear to be random scribblings, do in fact have the intention to create meaning. We can sometimes even recognize different types of 'text' in the forms which the marks take. It could be said, then, that we can see in the scribblings of very young children an attempt to create meaning with the skills which they have in their repertoire. It is likely too that children are experimenting with a form of communication which they have seen other people use.

A good example of this is the ghost story (Fig. 5.1) written by Jane, aged 3½ (Newman 1984). Since Jane composed aloud, we have the story in her own words:

> Mary Kate and Jane were playing outside.
> Then they went inside to watch TV.
> Then when they were watching TV they saw a scary thing – a ghost.
> So they hided under their covers.
> Then the ghost couldn't see them
> The ghost felt sad
> and he wrecked up the place.
> Then the ghost finally leaved.
> Then the girls lived happily ever after.

The rounded shapes to the left of the page are ghosts and are different from the horizontal marks which tell the story. There is a narrative, characters and a setting; the story ends with a resolution. She is beginning to learn that she can 'draw speech' and that there are boundaries between what is drawn and what is written, even though she cannot yet produce identifiable letters and words. Jane, it seems, is using writing for the purposes already important to her in her talk and in her play.

This example confirms the observations of Wolf and her colleagues (1988) that children seem to experiment with the range of symbol systems which they possess and that the process is one of active exploration rather than imitation. Children devise their own strategies for solving the problems which face them as they try to express meaning.

The realization of a direct correspondence between written and spoken words only comes gradually. Children will often show their emerging concept of writing by producing strings of letters as they mouth words like 'once upon a time' (Graves 1984: 223) and often assume that adults will understand what they have written. Case studies, such as that of Bissex (1980) indicate that very young children experiment with writing long before anyone teaches them. Bissex observed that her son used writing as an extension of both speech and drawing in order to categorize and label. The signs and captions which accompanied his drawings later became extended into more elaborate writing.

Figure 5.1 'Ghost Story' by Jane (aged 3½ years). (Reproduced from Newman [1984] by permission of the author and Scholastic–TAB Publications Ltd.)

In the early stages, writing tends to be a mere support for the drawing, and often lacks the drama and excitement which is so much more easily expressed by the young child in play or in pictures. By school age, most children seem to be able to distinguish between drawing and writing, yet until the child has mastered techniques of writing and literary style, drawing remains a powerful medium for expressing feeling well into the primary-school years. My elder son, Julian, and his friend, Nick, then 10 years old, spent many hours in their spare time writing serials for a magazine which they circulated amongst friends. Both authors and readers enjoyed sharing the incredible adventures in these cartoon stories. Figure 5.2 illustrates part of one episode in which the heroes, Phil and Robin, trapped on Despair Island, are not only pursued by dinosaurs but also find themselves in the path of an erupting volcano.

The narrative mode also appears in the symbolic play of preschool children. Smith argues that 'in some important respects the fantasy and socio-dramatic play of children can be thought of as the precursors of later imaginative story-writing or telling. There are structural similarities and some

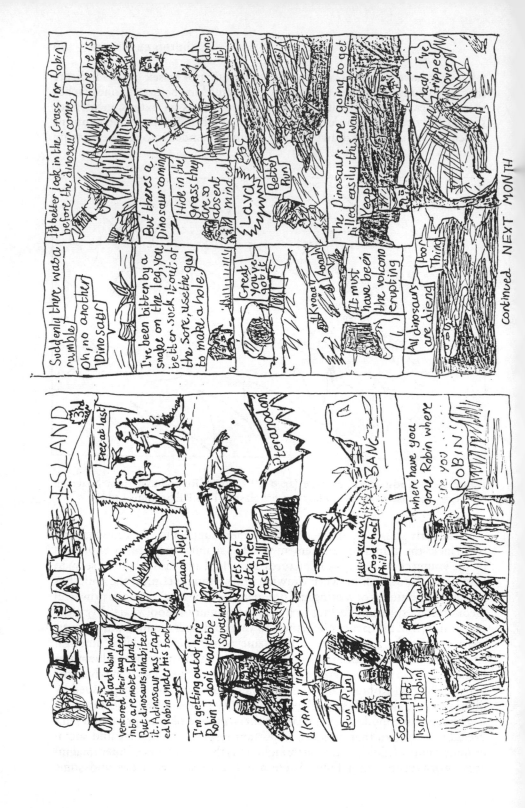

continued NEXT MONTH

psychologists have suggested direct links' (Smith 1984: 13). He notes the development of 'narrative-like' features in children's socio-dramatic play. Fantasy themes are often built round particular activities such as telephoning, going on a trip, healing/treating, and the children enact roles such as parent/child, husband/wife, doctor/nurse, which reveal some measure of social awareness and skill in portraying character.

Scarlett and Wolf (1979) gave preschool children props – a castle, a dragon, a royal family, toy animals and little trees – and noted the stories which they told. The researchers found that whereas children under the age of 3 tended to tell their stories through the actions of the toy figures, and could only sustain the story if they were in direct contact with the props, 4 year olds were much more likely to express their stories in linguistic ways; by telling the story in words, by creating dialogue and by explaining points to their audience.

Here is an example from observations of my 4-year-old son, Ben, as he integrates action, language and props in the creation of a narrative:

Ben has been given a large piece of white card and some coloured pens. He draws a series of jagged lines, carefully cuts them out and balances the structure on its end. 'This is a steep staircase', he says. 'Look! It stands by itself. Now, make me a little boy to go up the stairs.' His mother draws a small figure and cuts it out. Ben moves him up the stairs step by step and lets him fall from the top. He repeats this sequence several times and then hooks the arms of the paper doll over the top of the staircase.

'It's a castle now. He's standing at the top of the castle. Now I'm going to make a man.' He draws a second figure with enormous arms. 'He's a wizard and he's very strong. I'm going to give him a magic wand.' Ben carefully cuts round the wizard and wand and makes him flap his arms at the little boy on the battlements of the castle.

'He's swooping down on to the little boy. He's going to attack him. Look! He's magic too. He can fly!

'"Help! Help!" shouts the little boy.'

'"I am the strongest!" says the wizard in a deep voice.'

New props are added – a white bird which can rescue the little boy, a tall tower where he can hide. A series of short episodes is enacted in which the little boy always succeeds in overcoming the wicked intentions of the wizard.

What is happening in this series of little stories? Can they tell us anything about the stories which Ben will later write? Ben has chosen to enact events with the help of paper props and is satisfied with this means of communicating a story. Although there is no point at which he shows any inclination to have these narratives preserved in written form, I would argue that there are many parallels between this type of story and those which he will later write. For one thing, the characters engage in dialogue and Ben emphasizes their differences by tone of voice, gesture and facial expression, switching from one to the other with ease. He also shows empathy for his characters as they express mood, feeling and intention through their actions ('I'm going to knock you off the tower!') and their words ('Please don't hurt me. I'm only small!') They tell us what they are thinking and make predictions about what is going to happen next. Ben shows sensitivity to the needs of his audience (in this case his mother) when he stops from time to time to clarify a point ('This bird is going to fly away with the little boy') or explain an event ('His arms are hooked over the edge so he won't fall') and indicates his knowledge that there is a boundary between his narrative and the real world. Some of the events are random (the second paper figure only becomes a wizard because his arms happen to be very large and flappy) but once the scene is set, a narrative sequence unfolds and events move towards a resolution. Ben is showing awareness that he has control over the events and characters of his story, he has a hero who holds the episodes together, incidents in the story are linked and they lead to a resolution. He is developing the concept that a story has a structure (Applebee 1978) and a sense that language can capture events and delineate character.

A close study of this kind of activity can reveal much about the ways in which young children use the resources at their disposal in order to explore the themes which are so important to them. Children also seem to be developing a range of symbol systems – ways of expressing meaning which they will integrate into their writing at a later stage. In the next section of the chapter I discuss the ways in which children's facility in drawing, speech and play may later be integrated and extended as they learn to write.

The analysis of narrative structure

> We reveal ourselves directly or indirectly through all our narratives, polishing those we deem the best – either the clearest windows to our true selves or the most effective shutters over the same, depending on our personality. Either way, this self-revelation begins with the narratives we tell as children.
>
> (Peterson and McCabe 1983)

From a very early age children use conventions to mark their narratives. These include formal beginnings, formal endings, use of the past tense, use of a special story voice as well as the use of stock characters and events. It is out of these basic conventions that later evolve more elaborate strategies for creating a convincing narrative. The structural analysis of narratives told and written by children has given useful insights into the process of creating a satisfying story. Since Bartlett (1932) in his work on story recall observed that narratives have identifiable patterns, there have been numerous studies of narrative structure in socio-dramatic play, and in stories written and told by children. Recent studies (e.g. Galda 1984; Gardner 1980) indicate patterns of narrative structure in children's dramatic play; for example, by the age of 4, children readily differentiate between the voices of narrator and characters, and their play often concerns a central problem which is worked out through a sequence of logical events towards a resolution. Research shows that children gradually acquire expectations about the structure of a story. Even novice writers indicate that they have a basic sense of story (Applebee 1978; Gundlach 1982; Pitcher and Prelinger 1963) by giving their narratives settings, characters, actions and outcomes.

Applebee (1978) found that there are patterns in the growing complexity of the narratives told and written by children. Children progress, he argues, from a 'heap' of unconnected perceptions (a kind of stream of consciousness) to a more organized narrative which contains a central episode around which the story is built. Other writers (Botvin and Sutton-Smith 1977; Pradl 1979; Sutton-Smith 1979) also suggest that the concept of plot emerges gradually. Despite wide variation in the individual use of story, young children from 2 to 5 years tend to produce 'frame' stories – that is, stories which consist mainly of a beginning and an end – about stock characters who experience un-balancing and unresolved adventures. Older children will distribute aspects of their stories over the categories beginning, middle and end.

Systematic work on story grammars pioneered by Mandler and Johnson (1977) has been used to assess the developmental level of young writers. Mandler and Johnson suggest that a good story has four parts: a setting, beginning, development and an ending. The simplest complete story consists of a setting and an event structure. As Figure 5.3 shows, the event structure can be subdivided into an episode which contains a beginning leading to a development which finally causes the ending.

From the adult reader's point of view, if stories are 'grammatically' well formed, they are remembered better. Conversely, it takes adults longer to read and summarize scrambled stories than stories which conform to a logical sequence (Stein and Nezworski 1978). For children there are developmental differences. 6 and 7 year olds recall settings, initiating events and conse-quences more frequently than attempts to resolve the problem in a story; 9 and 10 year olds recall attempts to find a resolution equally well (Mandler and Johnson 1977). Young children rank consequences as being of more importance than initiating events; the reverse is true for older children (Stein and Glenn 1979).

Kroll and Anson (1984) analysed stories written by fifty-four 9 year olds and identified three main patterns:

1. Events are strung together in a linear fashion; there is a horizontal pattern in the sense that each episode is complete in itself
2. Events are connected by embedding; episodes are embedded rather than linked sequentially so that the outcome of a goal causes a new episode

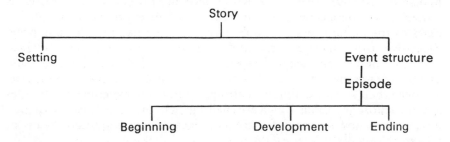

Figure 5.3   A story grammar adapted from Mandler and Johnson (1977).

3. A combination of linear and embedded episodes; such stories tend to be longer and more detailed.

They also note wide individual differences in children's capacity to develop characterization in a central hero or heroine, in the use of dialogue for differentiating character, and in the use of special linguistic devices which grow out of the story voice (e.g. use of literary phrases like 'atop a pinnacle of rock' or alliteration like 'the hissing snake'). They argue that these aspects of story structure may be used to evaluate writing ability and, more importantly, as guidelines in the development of children's mastery of the craft of writing.

Although the story grammar approach is quite different from approaches which focus on the content of what the child writes, its use confirms other research findings, especially those which deal with children's perception of the social world as expressed through the medium of narrative. Children seem to use conventions such as formal beginnings, formal endings, use of tenses and the device of dialogue, to mark their narratives. It is out of these basic conventions that evolve more elaborate strategies for creating a convincing narrative. Research studies indicate how the structural analysis of stories can complement studies which focus on content. Each approach indicates developmental changes in the ways that children understand events and characters drawn from real life or fiction, as well as a wide range of individual differences in competence. There would also seem to be scope for helping children to develop their competence as writers.

Writing and social role-taking

We have seen how children spontaneously create imaginary roles, actions and events, and how they co-ordinate sequential plans or narrative structures in their play, their drawing and their story-telling, sometimes alone but often in collaboration with others. This process continues once children have begun to express their narratives in *written* form. The skills of role-taking and empathy which develop throughout childhood (Flavell 1968; Light 1987) can be charted in the social awareness expressed in the themes which children create in their stories. Applebee (1978) and Britton (1970) argue that the creation of imaginative stories enhances children's capacity to understand the people and events in their social world since, in Britton's words, children as authors take 'the spectator role' in accounts of the experiences and interactions of their characters. Britton's argument goes like this. By distancing themselves from an experience, children not only represent the events which occurred but have also devised a system which may help them to make sense of past events and make predictions about similar events in the future. Through their stories, children create opportunities to experiment with roles and to explore situations which are challenging to them; they use the characters, actions and settings of their narratives as one important means of becoming socially aware.

But can we really know that children are using the writing process for these purposes? Some researchers, sceptical of Britton's model of children as writers, have tried to be more precise in charting the social and emotional development of young writers both in relation to other people and within the context of specific social situations.

In the Crediton Project (Wilkinson *et al.* 1980), a study which evaluated a variety of forms of written language in the classroom, the authors analysed, amongst other things, the development of 'affect' (their term for 'emotional, interpersonal and imaginative awareness') in stories written by 150 7, 11 and 13 year olds. The children were asked to write an autobiographical narrative, *The Happiest/Saddest Day of my Life*, and a fictional story in response to three photographs. The researchers investigated the social sensitivity of the young writers in relation to five categories: *the self* (awareness of own feelings and emotions); *other people* (awareness of others both in relation to self and as distinctive identities); *the reader* (the capacity of the writer to take into acount the perspective of the reader by giving relevant information or explaining points, sometimes through asides or in parenthesis); *the environment* (an awareness of physical and social surroundings, some sense of time and place, the use of context to create an effect), and *reality* (a knowledge of the distinction between fantasy and reality, between magical and logical thinking, an awareness of the literal-metaphorical aspects of experience).

Wilkinson *et al.* (1980) found age-related trends in self-awareness, social sensitivity and the ability to adapt to the needs of an audience. They found that 7 year olds did not on the whole express feeling in their writing and could be quite matter-of-fact about the most horrific of experiences. In the shortest story, one boy wrote simply: 'The saddest day was when my dog got knocked down.' This literal statement, lacking in introduction and without context, showed no self-analysis and no sense of the impact of the event on others. While this boy was at the extreme end of the spectrum, the general conclusion from the study was that 7 year olds did not express feeling explicitly, and had difficulties in describing their characters in any detail in order to make them 'come alive'. Awareness of audience was low, and very few cues were given to the reader as aids to visualizing the setting of the story. Over half of the 7 year olds gave no indication of their attitudes towards the characters in their stories; only five of them quoted the direct speech of others; only two showed awareness of the feelings of others. On the whole, there was very little description of the setting and the treatment of the stories was literal rather than metaphorical. By contrast, 10 and 13 year olds produced more realistic themes than 7 year olds with less reliance on fantasy; but at the same time these older children dealt with the themes in a more imaginative way, through sensitivity to the feelings of their characters and awareness of the needs of their audience. There were also developmental trends in the ability to take the other person's point of view and the ability to describe social relationships among characters.

One explanation for the egocentric nature of the writing produced by the 7 year olds in the Crediton Project may be due to the constraints of the writing

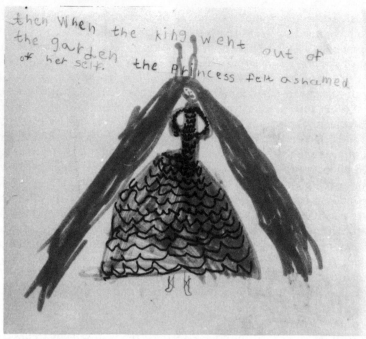

Figure 5.4 'The Princess' by Jenny (aged 6 years).

task itself. Although the children in this study were asked to write in familiar surroundings at a time when creative writing normally took place, we do not know how they perceived the task. The titles were supplied by the research team, the stories were analysed outside the classroom setting, and there is no record of any talk which took place while the children wrote or as they reflected on what they had written. Although the team comment at length on the need to take account of the social context in which writing is done, their concern is not reflected in the design of the research itself.

Quite a different approach to the study of children's writing was adopted by a team of researchers in New Hampshire (Graves 1983). Their work demonstrated that writing researchers who focus on the child in the context where writing takes place are likely to reach different conclusions from those who do not. Graves would have viewed the short piece on the death of the 7 year old's dog as a first draft and would have encouraged the child to explore his own feelings about that day in his life, about what he said, what other people did, how he had come to terms with the event now. The final account might well have been very different from the brief sentence which is reproduced by Wilkinson and his team.

The following example, written by 6-year-old Jenny, illustrates how much more we can learn from a child's story when we know something of the child's interests at home and at school, her ideas on writing, the responses of her audience and the context in which she writes. Jenny has already developed a great love of books since her parents read to her regularly. Her teacher has created a classroom environment where children are accustomed to listen to stories and are encouraged to share and comment on one another's writing. Favourite pieces are bound by the teacher and placed in the library alongside published books. In *The Princess* Jenny uses characters from the fairy tale world in order to explore what happens when a child confronts angry adult figures. Her central character, the princess, has to cope with feelings of shame when she talks back to a father who finds it hard to admit that he might be mistaken; her situation becomes even more disturbing when she discovers that she has accidentally eaten a witch's home (Fig. 5.4).

THE PRINCESS
Once upon a time there lived a princess one day the princess was walking in her garden. Suddenly she saw two apple trees in her garden and she said to herself those trees weren't there yesterday. Then she ran to tell the king what she had seen. The king said nonsense but the princess said it is true come and see and the king did. When the princess led the king out of the castle and the king said oh and the princess said see and the king said don't speak to me like that. then when the king went right out of the garden the princess felt ashamed of herself. then the princess looked at the trees one more time. then the princess ate all the apples all up and when she ate the last apple a witch popped out of the apple. then the princess felt very frihtened she began to shake then the witch said to the princess why did you eat my home said the witch the

princess felt more frightened and then the witch took a potion and then she drank the potion and she died.
THE END

Illustrations are used to enhance the words which describe her characters and set the scene, but the writing also achieves effective description and expression on its own. Jenny acknowledges her sources, as the following verbatim quote from an interview with her shows:

> The way the princess has such long hair – that's from Rapunzel ... Well, the prince comes to a forest where he sees the tower and a witch come so he hides in a tree and the witch says, 'Rapunzel, Rapunzel, let down your hair'. And Rapunzel lets down her hair and she climbs up it and she's a prisoner in the tower ... The apples come from Snow White because she eats an apple which has poison in it. The *apples* come from that but the apple trees don't. (The witch?) In all the fairy tales that I know of, they don't have witches popping out of apples. *I* think most of it all up.

She is satisfied with the way in which she freed the princess from danger. Classmates also found the content of the story pleasing ('I like when the witch drinks the poison because I think the witch might have turned a bit nasty to the princess'), but would have liked to have had more information about motives ('Why did the witch take the potion?') and outcomes ('What happened to the princess?' and 'Who died?'). An older child would have devised a more elaborate plot development and a less abrupt ending.

Children in this classroom, where talk about writing is encouraged, are also interested in speculating about alternative endings:

> *Ruth*: A fairy came and turned the witch into a frog. She got a prince and they went to get married.
> *Francis*: I'd have said, the king came back and said to the witch, 'You must leave this garden'. And she did. And then she went into the castle and a guard saw her and the guards put her in jail.

But Jenny is already thinking ahead to her next story: 'I've started writing a story at home and it's about when the parents go to bed and all the fruit come to life. I got the idea from *Sesame Street*...'

What children tell us about their writing

How much can children actually tell us about their own experience as authors? I interviewed junior school children about how they saw themselves as authors, about the influences on their writing, and about their concepts of what made a good story (Cowie 1985). This selection of their viewpoints reveals some of the richness and variety with which the writing process is experienced by children.

I find stories take me into another world. They help me understand other people's points of view and also my own life. It is interesting through story to go into another country or go back in time.

(Mark, aged 10)

I like adventures and magic because they make me shiver inside.

(Joanna, aged 9)

A loving part, a wicked part and a nice part at the end makes a very good story.

(Owen, aged 9)

Sometimes I like to write what's happened and put myself in the position of another person and see how they feel.

(Elizabeth, aged 9)

Some story-writing is playful – a humorous commentary on life using themes from literature, comics and television in a series of adventures where fictional characters and real-life people intermingle. This kind of action-packed writing is close to the 'theatre imagination' described by Sutton-Smith which in his view 'originates that revitalization of everyday living' (Sutton-Smith 1988: 9) that is at the heart of play, of carnival, of recreation and of leisure. Children often express great pleasure in writing these adventures and in sharing them with one another. In order to understand their meaning fully, the reader needs to know something of the culture shared by the children who enjoy them so much. For example, Jason and his friends draw on their shared experience of popular television themes when they create their own stories:

I get my ideas from cartoons – strength and running, power and speed. We change the names or the speed and strength . . . Sometimes I put them all in one story – a gang of Roadrunners and a gang of Superstrong men – then they fight one very strong person.

Collaborative fantasy play, so important in the preschool years, continues to be a productive source of ideas. For example, Mark, aged 9, describes how his story grew out of a game which he and two friends devised at break:

It was me and Owen and Adam. I was thinking of the Stukas' invasion at the Battle of Britain. We thought of Stukas coming in and we ran to the guns to get the Stukas away. There were 256 planes and we were trying to shoot them down with four guns per plane. We destroyed 150 of them and then some other people helped us shoot them.

Jon, aged 10, a prolific writer of space stories which are very popular with his peers, enjoys exploring his imaginary world in which he gives detailed descriptions of characters ('slimy green tetrapods') and settings ('the bed that Jargon Plage lay on was made of plonum, a kind of metal'). He finds everyday human life 'limiting' and positively revels in the opportunity to take part in extravagant, impossible adventures on other planets.

Some children, by contrast, describe a quieter, more reflective aspect of the world of imagination, perhaps in 'a magic land', in 'a country far away' or in 'an enchanted world', often, but not always, drawing on their reading for inspiration:

> I like thinking about the sky and the colours of the sky ... I like thinking about the clouds and if I was floating in the air – quiet, lonely.
>
> (Claire, aged 8)

> I think writing's a lovely quiet thing and you can get your brain stuck into it. You can do exciting things, then it goes down to soft things like dragonflies and love affairs. My favourite is soft things ... It's lovely once you're given a subject. You write words down, find books to read ... I think of myself as an author. I take lots of imaginative words and jumble them up. I got an idea from *The Trumpet of the Swan, The Lion, the Witch and the Wardrobe* and *Danny*. One's loving, one's dramatic, and one has one side loving and one side wicked – that's a good combination.
>
> (Owen, aged 9)

The settings of these stories need not always be imaginary. Mark, aged 10, finds his sources in factual books and uses the information to help him enter into another period of time:

> Sometimes I doodle away on a piece of paper for my own enjoyment, for example about trains. I think that I'm Stephenson and going down the Liverpool–Manchester Railway. I may not write it on paper. I may write it in my mind. It's like taking lots and lots of photographs and then they come out of your mouth ... I often think these ideas in bed.

James also consults an adult for a first-hand account of wartime experience so that his story will be more authentic:

> I like *Colditz*. I got more thoughts on that one. I've seen loads of films and I have books on escape. My grandpa was in the war and I ask him what he did and ask what places he worked on. One day I asked him about D-Day ... I like writing about war more than feeling. I prefer escape – the parts where your heart stops and the hero is just about to be shot!

Other children describe how writing helps them to understand themselves and others. To some, writing has a therapeutic effect as a way of coming to terms with painful experiences like the death of a pet or being afraid at night. One 9 year old spoke of

> stories my mum says I shouldn't write because they're really sad – dogs and cats dying of a fever. I have some in my wardrobe. I won't read them because they're so sad but I feel better when I've written them down.

8-year-old Darren describes how he learnt about himself by writing about an angry outburst:

> I'm very pleased with that story. It tells you a lot – how you get angry, why you get angry, what happens when you get angry – and it tells you what you do – swear, punch, kick, stamp, be sent to bed.

In addition to experiencing relief at distancing himself from the angry feelings, Darren reports that he uses writing in order to achieve a long-term perspective on his own development:

> When I'm 18, I'll look back to when I was 8 and see what I wrote. I would think that I was doing interesting things – finding birds, watching kestrels and kites and finding acorns.

His problem seems to be finding time to write down all the ideas with which his mind teems:

> I like writing about ghosts, adventures, animals and birds, and pirates. Ghosts are the best. I'm writing one now about *The House of Nightmare* in class. It's a made-up story. I like writing about the army, space, underground in the mine, dinosaurs, earthquakes and volcanoes – hot slurping mud! And I like reading books. They give me ideas.

Michelle, however, is not so much concerned to write a commentary on her own life as to deepen her understanding of other people:

> I have an idea and I like other people to imagine what I'm trying to make them imagine, so they can see and feel in their mind what I've seen ... When a character starts talking, I like to feel that I'm that character and that the others are talking to me.
>
> (Michelle, aged 10)

Michelle can not only describe how she enters into a role and interacts with the characters whom she has created, but she is also concerned to make her characters come alive for her audience:

> I've got to sit down and think: for example, if I'm writing about a storm, I think how many people, what are their names. Are they interesting people? Are they rich and spoilt or are they poor people? I put information about their background in, write down what they *are*, not just their names. Then you have a picture of that person.

These extracts from conversations with young writers give some sense of the variety of thoughts, feelings and sheer enjoyment which children bring to the task of creating a narrative and may complement those studies which focus only on the written piece.

Creating an environment where writing may flourish

Parents play a key role in helping their children to develop as writers since the language abilities developed in the preschool years seem to be crucial for the later development of reading and writing. Parents can foster and encourage the development of talk, fantasy play and drawing, and so provide the kind of home environment where the imagination may flourish. They can read both fiction and non-fiction with children, making use of a wide range of texts and doing it not only for enjoyment (although this is important) but also with purpose, since from reading, as from their own make-believe play, children can discover that good stories enrich the imagination, develop understanding and empathy, and generate ideas (Tucker 1981; Wade 1984).

Later, adults can help children of school age to develop the craft of writing – for example, how to begin and end stories, how to develop character, how to set a scene. Children are very responsive to the idea that the techniques of writing can be learned (Harris and Wilkinson 1986; Scardamalia, Bereiter and Goelman 1982). By looking systematically at texts written by children, teachers can identify the problems involved in producing a piece of writing and formulate specific strategies to help the child. At the same time, by working collaboratively on beginnings and endings, by experimenting with alternatives, by sharing suspense techniques and devices for creating effective characters, children can discover for themselves that writing is a craft which they can master.

Many young writers need time to experiment during the drafting phase of the writing process. A collaborative environment in the classroom is most helpful for developing in children a sense of audience and enabling them to have control over their own writing processes (Graves 1983; Cowie and Hanrott 1984). Teachers have found it helpful to create a classroom environment where children write for a range of readers (perhaps writing stories for younger children or creating a class magazine for peers) not just the class teacher, and where there is a sense of a writing community. Teachers can also develop their own craft by writing with the children and sharing experiences, both of successful writing and of writing blocks. Many teachers find that the word processor can give children confidence in their ability to engage in the process of drafting, revising and editing by giving them scope to add details of a description, or to clarify points in the narrative which are unclear to the reader.

Perhaps the most important aspect of the adult's role, however, lies in the capacity to listen to what children have to say about writing and to enter into the world of imagination which children create in their stories. Listening to children's views on writing can give insights into their social and emotional life, the issues which concern them and the anxieties which they face. It is surely by listening to them and responding to the themes which they create in their stories that we can best help them to develop a voice and a sense that what they have to say matters.

References

Applebee, A. N. (1978). *The Child's Concept of Story*. Chicago, University of Chicago Press.

Bartlett, F. C. (1932). *Remembering*. Cambridge, Cambridge University Press.

Bissex, G. (1980). *GNYS AT WRK: A Child Learns to Read and Write*. Cambridge, Mass., Harvard University Press.

Botvin, G. and Sutton-Smith, B. (1977). 'The development of structural complexity in children's fantasy narratives'. *Developmental Psychology*, 13(4): 377–88.

Britton, J. N. (1970). *Language and Learning*. Harmondsworth, Penguin.

Bruner, J. S. and Haste, H. (1987). *Making Sense*. London, Methuen.

Clay, M. (1975). *What Did I Write?* Auckland, Heinemann.

Cowie, H. (1985). 'An approach to the evaluation of children's narrative writing'. Unpublished Ph. D. Thesis, University of London Institute of Education, London.

Cowie, H. and Hanrott, H. (1984). 'The writing community: a case study of one junior school class', in H. Cowie (ed.), *The Development of Children's Imaginative Writing*. London, Croom Helm.

Ferreiro, E. and Teberesky, A. (1982). *Literacy Before Schooling*. Exeter, NH, Heinemann.

Flavell, J. (1968). *The Development of Role-taking and Communication*. New York, John Wiley.

Galda, L. (1984). 'Narrative competence: play, story-telling and story-comprehension', in A. Pellegrini and T. Yawkey (eds.), *The Development of Oral and Written Language in Social Contexts*. Norwood, NJ, Ablex.

Gardner, H. (1980). *Artful Scribbles*. New York, Basic Books.

Graves, D. H. (1983). *Writing: Teachers and Children at Work*. Exeter, NH, Heinemann.

(1984). 'Patterns of child control of the writing process', in H. Cowie (ed.), *The Development of Children's Imaginative Writing*. London, Croom Helm.

Gundlach, R. A. (1982). 'Children as writers: the beginning of learning to write', in M. Nystrand (ed.), *What Writers Know*. New York, Academic Press.

Harris, J. and Wilkinson, J. (1986). *Reading Children's Writing*. London, Allen & Unwin.

Kroll, B. and Anson, C. (1984). 'Analysing structure in children's fictional narratives', in H. Cowie (ed.), *The Development of Children's Imaginative Writing*. London, Croom Helm.

Light, P. (1987). 'Taking roles', in J. S. Bruner and H. Haste (eds.), *Making Sense*. New York, Methuen.

Mandler, J. and Johnson, N. (1977). 'Remembrance of things parsed: story structure and recall'. *Cognitive Psychology*, 9: 111–51.

Newman, J. (1984). *The Craft of Children's Writing*. New York, Scholastic Book Services.

Peterson, C. and McCabe, A. (1983). *Developmental Psycholinguistics: Three Ways of Looking at a Child's Narrative*. New York, Plenum.

Pitcher, E. and Prelinger, E. (1963). *Children Tell Stories: An Analysis of Fantasy*. New York, International University Press.

Pradl, G. M. (1979). 'Learning how to begin and end a story'. *Language Arts*, 56(1).

Scardamalia, M., Bereiter, C. and Goelman, H. (1982). 'The role of production factors in writing ability', in M. Nystrand (ed.), *What Writers Know*. New York. Academic Press.

Scarlett, G. and Wolf, D. (1979). 'When it's only make-believe; the construction of a boundary between fantasy and reality in story-telling', in H. Gardner and E. Winner (eds.), *Fact, Fiction and Fantasy in Childhood*. San Francisco, Jossey-Bass.

Smith, P. K. (1984). 'The relevance of fantasy play for development in young children', in H. Cowie (ed.), *The Development of Children's Imaginative Writing*. London, Croom Helm.

Stein, N. L. and Glenn, C. (1979). 'An analysis of story comprehension in elementary school children', in R. Freedle (ed.), *New Directions in Discourse Processing*. Hillsdale, NJ, Ablex.

Stein, N. L. and Nezworski, M. T. (1978). 'The effect of organisation and instructional set on story memory'. *Discourse Processes*, 1: 177–93.

Sutton-Smith, B. (1979). 'Presentation and representation in children's fictional narrative', in E. Winner and H. Gardner (eds.), *Fact, Fiction and Fantasy in Childhood*. San Francisco, Jossey Bass.

(1988). 'In search of the imagination', in K. Egan and D. Nadaner (eds.), *Imagination and Education*. Milton Keynes, Open University Press.

Tucker, N. (1981). *The Child and the Book*. Cambridge, Cambridge University Press.

Vygotsky, L. (1978). *Mind in Society*. Ed. by M. Cole, V. John-Steiner, S. Scribner and E. Souberman. Cambridge, Mass., Harvard University Press.

Wade, B. (1984). *Story at Home and in School*. Birmingham, University of Birmingham, Faculty of Education, Educational Review.

Wells, C. G. (1985). 'Pre-school literacy-related activities', in D. Olson, N. Torrance and A. Hildyard (eds.), *Literacy, Language and Learning*. Cambridge, Cambridge University Press.

Wilkinson, A., Barnsley, G., Hanna, P. and Swan, M. (1980). *Assessing Language Development*. Oxford, Oxford University Press.

Wolf, D., Davidson, L., Davis, M., Walters, J., Hodges, M. and Scripp, L. (1988). 'Affective and social dimensions of early education', in A. Pellegrini (ed.), *Psychological Bases for Early Education*. Chichester, John Wiley.

6
Sculpture: the development of representational concepts in a three-dimensional medium

Claire Golomb

The study of child art

The last 100 years have seen a considerable interest in child art and a growing appreciation, among psychologists as well as artists, for the simple forms that characterize early representational efforts. Within the domain of child art, investigators have focused almost exclusively on children's drawings (Arnheim 1974; Burt 1921; Eng 1931; Freeman 1980; Gardner 1980; Goodenough 1926; Harris 1963; Kerschensteiner 1905; Luquet 1913, 1927; Piaget and Inhelder 1956; Rouma 1912; Wilson and Wilson 1982; see also Cox, Chapter 3 of this volume). The most likely reason for this singular concern with drawings can be sought, at least in part, in the ease with which drawings can be solicited, collected and stored. A further restriction seems to have guided much of the research devoted to child art, namely a special concern for the representation of the human figure. Perhaps the desire to make drawings amenable to a quantitative analysis has led to the emphasis on the drawn human figure. Given that with age a child's drawing shows increasing detail, richness and eventual approximation to adult standards, it is not surprising that scoring systems based on the number of parts and the quality of the representation have been developed. Such instruments were designed to analyse the drawings from a cognitive developmental perspective, that is for what they can tell us about a child's mental maturity. While investigators differ in their choice of explanatory concepts designed to account for age-related changes, there is widespread agreement that drawings provide a record of representational problem-solving in the graphic domain: Maureen Cox adopts this approach in Chapter 3 of the present volume. Disagreements concerning the meaning of the observed changes in drawing style reflect the diverse theoretical orientations of researchers who have dominated this field of enquiry. Thus, for example, both Goodenough (1926) and Harris (1963) view drawing development in terms of the child's acquisition of specific concepts, in the case of the human figure drawing, the concept of man or person, while Piaget and Inhelder (1956) consider drawings as indicators of the child's developing spatial-geometrical concepts. Arnheim (1974) invokes the law of differentiation and the tendency toward simplicity as major determinants of the child's evolving graphic logic, while Freeman (1980) analyses children's immature drawing styles mainly in terms of production problems. Unlike the cognitive emphasis of the above-mentioned authors, Wilson and Wilson (1982) view drawing development essentially as a social phenomenon, a function of peer influence in the early years, and a product of culturally dominant styles at a later phase. Clearly, this is not an attempt to provide an exhaustive account of important positions in the field, but merely a listing of major positions that have influenced the direction research has taken over many decades.

All students of child art focus on the unique forms drawing development takes in early stages of development. They attempt to account for what appear to be developmental markers of the child art style, for example the early graphic models of global, tadpole and open-trunk humans. Much of the debate on the meaning of young children's drawings has focused on the child's graphic limitations, most clearly seen in his deficient handling of the missing third dimension. Thus, for example, attention has been called to the so-called transparency of a drawing that depicts the inside of an object not directly visible to an outside observer, or to the failure to eliminate lines when objects overlap each other. When children attempt to portray more than a single view of an object, for example a cube, the different faces do not line up properly, and such errors have usually been interpreted in terms of cognitive deficits rather than technical naïveté. Given the inherent restrictions of the flat medium, all early representations limit their depiction to a single side or face of the object, for example in the case of humans – the frontal view, and for most animals – the side view. Another early childish tendency or error is often described as the horizontal–vertical bias that leads to such oddities as a chimney drawn at a right angle to the slanted roof-line instead of being drawn as a vertical upright.

I have mentioned but a few of the peculiarities of child art which follow directly from the nature of the two-dimensional graphic medium. These characteristics of child and naïve adult art reveal how two-dimensional graphic equivalents come to represent the three-dimensional object. In the two-dimensional medium of drawing and painting, children like adults face an acute problem of how to represent three dimensional space and the many sides of an object with materials that bear no resemblance to the world that is to be portrayed. The differences between the object to be represented and the medium of paper, pencil, crayon and magic marker are indeed profound. As our individual and collective histories have shown us, we learn to compensate for the deficiencies of the medium and to use its properties in ways that create an essentially imaginary world, one that comes into existence through the magic of lines and the use of colour.

It has taken psychologists many decades to understand that representation is not to be mistaken for the imitation of nature in any literal sense, and that art, even child art, is not intent on copying *per se*. Theories of graphic representation could gain in explanatory power if they also considered development in three-dimensional media. A comparison of two- and three-dimensional representational strategies could highlight similarities as well as differences among the two domains, and thus help tease apart effects that are medium-specific from those that are a function of the child's immature cognitive level, variables that, most commonly, are confounded in the study of children's drawings. Thus, for example, the question whether the 'naïve' drawings of young children reflect the child's immature and distorted spatial conception or represent an early and reasonable graphic solution can best be examined by comparing work done in both domains. By exploring different media we might be in a better position to choose between a view that emphasizes cognitive immaturity (Harris 1963; Piaget and Inhelder, 1956) and one that speaks to the graphic logic of early representations (Arnheim 1974; Golomb 1974).

Sculpture and modelling

Unlike the fairly long tradition of examining children's drawings, the study of the development of sculpture and modelling has lagged far behind. In the beginning of this century, several students of child art reported their findings on children's modelling of the human figure, but these studies lacked the necessary experimental and statistical controls (Martin 1932; Matz 1912; Wulff 1932). The first systematic exploration of the development of three-dimensional concepts and modelling skills in young children's representation of the human figure was published in the 1970s (Golomb 1972, 1973, 1974). The publications that have appeared since that time are few in number; their focus is primarily pedagogical, that is to facilitate the use of the medium in creative and expressive ways (Burton 1981; Grossman 1980), or they limit themselves to a mere listing of body parts and the ages at which they are modelled (Brown 1975). By and large, a review of the published literature indicates that the development of three-dimensional representation is a much neglected area. Apparently, researchers have simply skipped over this field of enquiry.

This is a regrettable state of affairs since exploring the development of modelling in clay or Plasticine is important in its *own right*, and not merely as a means for resolving controversies about drawing development. Sculpting affords the artist the opportunity to consider the totality of the object and to represent its major aspects. Both the artist and the viewer are free to vary their position *vis-à-vis* a sculpture which, unlike a drawing, can be viewed from diverse angles. Thus a sculpture can offer a more comprehensive statement about the nature of the object than a drawing thereof.

In this domain, a series of important questions need to be addressed: What is the general course of differentiation in the plastic medium? Does representation proceed from an early undifferentiated state to the use of at first one, then two, and lastly three dimensions, or are three-dimensional concepts used from the very beginning, albeit in a primitive form? If children have a basic notion of three-dimensionality which they bring to clay and Playdough, what does it consist of? Are they more likely to 'imitate' the volumetric properties of the object when working with clay? What awareness do children have of the possibilities this medium can afford them to represent quite directly the 'inside' and the 'outside', the 'front' and the 'back' view of an object? Are children more likely to represent the different sides of an object in clay than in drawing, or are they content with the canonical orientation that represents the single view that best captures the essential characteristics of the object? Since modelling with clay or Playdough can lend itself to the making of real objects, and a sculpture can function as a symbolic play object, do children think of their sculpture as a miniature copy of the object, or do they conceive of it as a 'stand-in' for the real object? If it is the latter, what requirements does the representation have to meet, and how do the criteria for such a representation change with experience and practice? Unlike the apparent permanence or fixity of a drawn figure, the child who models a figure with clay, Plasticine or Playdough can, quite easily, change his creation. Given the revisability of these media, and the latitude for ongoing experimentation, does the child avail himself of this opportunity to shape the material until it meets his expectations? Finally, given the active exploration of the medium that involves such major sensory modalities as vision, touch and smell, does this bodily involvement lead to products that have a deeper emotional significance for the child than is the case for drawing? To most of these questions, and these are central questions, we do not, as yet, have answers, but we have gained some understanding of young children's early representational concepts from a study I conducted, in which I focused on the modelling of the human figure.

Modelling the human figure

When 2 year olds are presented with Playdough (or Plasticine, provided it is soft and pliable) and asked to make a doll, a mummy, or a daddy, they don't seem to comprehend the request. They may finger the dough, pinch it, squeeze it a bit, transfer it to the other hand, and then offer the dough essentially unchanged to the experimenter. A little later, the toddlers may act more vigorously on the medium, stretching, pounding and flattening it. At this point, they tend to incorporate the dough into their games, for example by squeezing it into a car or pretending to eat it. The early exploration of this medium is action-oriented, it is merely action *on* and *with* the dough, and it does not yet lead to any effort to represent an object. The child's behaviour clearly indicates that she does not yet conceive of such a possibility. Her actions may become symbolic as when a piece of dough is used as a substitute object for a pretence play episode, for example moving the dough piece across the table and making motor sounds, or lifting the blob of dough in imitation of drinking. Such imitative actions, however, do not treat the Playdough as a medium for plastic representation.

Within the span of only a few months, however, the pre-representational child makes the transition from the passive and aimless handling of the Playdough to a more active exploration of the material, and finally to representation proper. On this course, the child first employs quite primitive pseudo-representational devices such as romancing about an undifferentiated blob of Playdough or using gestures that imitate an action. A more deliberate approach to the representational medium can be seen when the child inspects the incidental shape the material has taken on while being handled. Scrutinizing the shape and searching for some similarity to an object in the real world, the child determines the meaning of the clay object by 'reading-off' what it might be. Finally, the child also verbally designates those parts that have not been modelled. All of these pre-representational devices tend to ignore the task set by the experimenter, namely to represent a specific object. Whatever actions on the medium the child may have used, they have not produced a visible likeness to the designated object, and he uses verbal comments and imitative actions to *substitute* for representation proper.

Nevertheless, the use of such devices suggests that the toddler or preschooler has some intuition that someone other than the child could 'make' something out of Playdough. As yet, the child doesn't quite know what needs to be done or how the dough-blob ought to look. In the meantime, however, his explorations have become more deliberate and skilful, and using a rolling motion the child may create something that looks like a snake or a sausage, and using a rotational movement, a ball-like shape results, both of which become important elements for the construction of figures and other objects. Such discoveries of how specific actions can yield identifiable shapes now facilitate the *transition* to representation proper, beginnings of which we see at approximately the age of 3 years. My observations indicate that this is a period of readiness, children show an eagerness to explore the three-dimensional medium and a capacity for fast learning. The child's explorations of the Playdough or Plasticine medium have led to such deliberate actions as rolling the dough, shaping an upright standing column, flattening the dough to pancake shapes, and the making of balls.

What are the first models of a human which the young child evolves in this medium? My study of 300 children, ranging in age from 2.4 to 7.4, identifies the evolution of three different models which children discover quite independently: (1) the upright standing column, (2) the ball or slab of dough with facial features and (3) the array of separate parts which consists mainly of facial features, but occasionally also includes limbs.

The most widespread of the early types of figure is a lengthened blob of dough, crudely shaped, held up in the air or placed on the table so that its position is upright, and the verticality of the figure emphasized (Fig. 6.1). It is a primitive upright column, little modelling has been performed, and in the majority of cases the major parts of the figure, namely the head, tummy and legs are supplied by words. The verbal designation and localization of parts

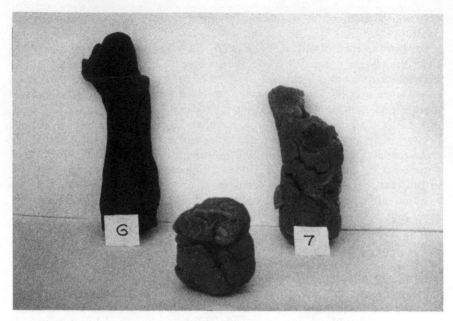

Figure 6.1

always corresponds to the actual spatial position of the parts, and it follows a top-to-bottom order. No particular aspect is singled out, the front and rear parts of the figure are essentially undifferentiated. We can infer the general conception which underlies this model of a human, namely the representational concept of verticality and uprightness.

A second type of figure that is frequently employed consists of a ball or a blob of flattened Playdough with facial features scratched on the surface, poked out, or added separately (Fig. 6.2). The child also makes use of ready-made marks and blemishes in the Playdough which can be interpreted according to their particular location on the figure, for example a mouth. By inscribing or attaching facial features, a surface or side of the figure has been singled out to represent the frontal aspect, an acknowledgement of the significance of the asymmetry that characterizes the human body. This global figure lacks the properties of verticality and uprightness, and relies on the facial features as the defining attributes of the human figure. A global-spheric concept underlies this representation of a human.

The third type of figure consists of an array of single facial features. The parts are separately formed and assembled on the table, without the benefit of the Playdough background, base or contour; nevertheless, the spatial orientation of the parts to each other is well preserved (Fig. 6.3). One may assume that the surface on which such parts as eyes, nose, mouth and legs are laid out provides the background for the figure, which is implicitly incorporated into the representation. This model is used less frequently. Perhaps a one-

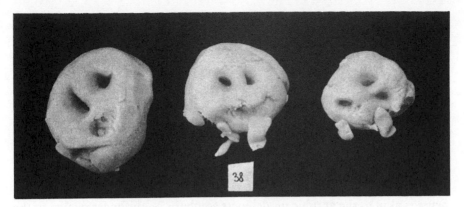

Figure 6.2

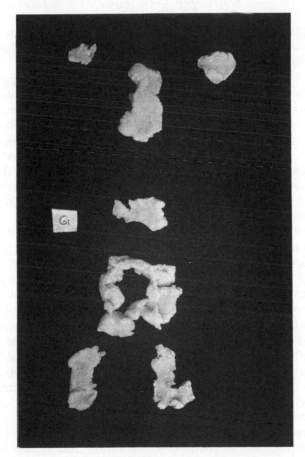

Figure 6.3

dimensional concept underlies this representation in which parts are treated as 'points'.

These three types of figure appear to evolve along separate lines, achieving differentiation of its parts either by a process of *addition* or by *internal subdivision* of the figure. Thus the column develops into a more differentiated figure either by an internal subdivision of its parts or by the addition of a small head on top of the column-body (Figs. 6.4 and 6.5). The blob with facial features sprouts legs and sometimes arms and is commonly known as the tadpole man (Figs. 6.6 and 6.7), while the lay-out model develops into a linear or graphic model, borrowing concepts and procedures from drawing (Figs. 6.8 and 6.9). In this case, the child seems to 'draw' the Playdough figure by outlining head and body with thin strips of Plasticine or Playdough. The stick figure is akin to the graphic model in its emphasis on the linear quality of the human (Fig. 6.10).

Additional practice yields greater modelling competence; figures are even further differentiated so that now head, body, arms and legs can be clearly distinguished (Figs. 6.11 and 6.12). However, such fine detail as facial features is often omitted, and many of the figures are faceless. Now, most sculptures are constructed via the addition process, and fewer children model a one-unit figure by internally subdividing its major parts.

The actual procedures of constructing a figure can vary significantly: we find *rounded-spheric shapes* that are carefully attached, but also *flattened asymmetrical pieces* that are, as it were, pasted onto the figure. While most figures are constructed in either a top-to-bottom or bottom-to-top sequence, some children begin their sculpture from the *middle*. Children may construct their figure in a piecemeal fashion, each time modelling a part and adding it to the evolving structure, or they may first create and label all of the parts and only then assemble them into a coherent structure. Thus construction sequences tend to vary considerably. The sculptures differ also in their orientation, either standing upright or lying down. Interestingly, the request to model a snowman yielded mostly upright standing figures, and if the mummy or daddy was modelled *after* the snowman, the result was a significant increase in upright standing humans (Fig. 6.13).

Until age 5 years, children tend to concentrate on the frontal plane of the figure, modelling facial features, belly-buttons, and occasionally hair. That the back is not simply forgotten can be seen in the behaviour of a 3 year 10 months old preschooler who made a global figure with facial features, turned it over and said, 'Now his back on – that's all done.' Among the 5 year olds, attention to the back part increases somewhat in frequency as subjects begin to turn the figure over and model its back lightly. Not surprisingly, the frontal part remains the major focus of children's modelling activity. Attention to the frontal aspect of the human figure indicates an awareness of the significant asymmetry between the front and the back, with the frontal part displaying the major organs of perception. These organs and their frontal orientation play a significant role in social communication and human locomotion. When visual representation is called for, all of these factors single the frontal

Figure 6.4

Figure 6.5

Figure 6.6

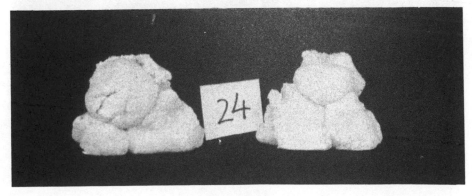

Figure 6.7

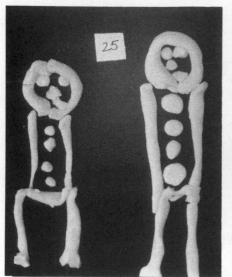

Figure 6.8

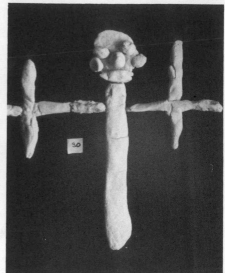

Figure 6.10

Figure 6.9

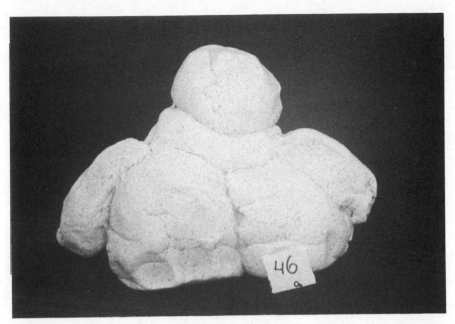

Figure 6.11

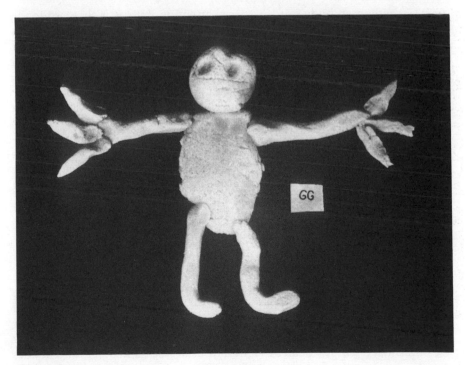

Figure 6.12

Figure 6.13

part of the human body out for special attention. Interestingly, despite the saliency of the frontal parts, the order in which children acquire the terms 'front' and 'back' indicates the lexical priority of the latter over the former (Leehey and Carey 1978). Apparently, visual and verbal modes of thinking do not always overlap. Finally, when considering the reasons for the relative neglect of the back part of the modelled figure, we ought to take note of the children's limited experience with modelling. Preliminary findings of a pilot study suggest that when children are asked to model a seated or a kneeling person, other aspects of the body can become the focus of attention. Furthermore, when such featureless symmetrical objects as a cup or a boat are modelled with Playdough, children attend to the object as a whole; in the case of the cup, the Playdough mass is rotated, turned evenly around the indenting thumb, indicating a concern with all the aspects or sides of the cup.

Conclusion

It would thus seem somewhat premature to conclude from the preference given to the frontal part of the human figure that we are faced with an intrinsic cognitive limitation in the child's three-dimensional conception of representation with clay. With further practice children might well discover additional possibilities that are *unique* to the three-dimensional medium, for example that a sculpture can be viewed from all sides, and that the artist does not have to restrict herself to a single viewing position. Such a working through of the possibilities of this medium of representation might have significant implications for the child's understanding of the nature of the object and of the symbolic activity of creating equivalences. Such 'working through' may affect not only the child's cognitive and artistic development but, perhaps, also his personal sense of self. To see oneself as a true maker in the basic sense of creating shapes, involves the mind, the heart and the body. Because of the revisability of the medium, it offers the child new opportunities *not* available in the medium of drawing. The tactile contact with the material fosters a more intimate involvement in the making process and a special appreciation for volumes and surfaces. Modelling also requires more persistence and a 'rethinking' about the object to be represented, and it may well lead to a deeper understanding of the object and of the self. In a culture that provides much visual information in the passive mode of watching television or viewing comic strips, modelling in clay encourages an active and constructive approach to the world and a different experience of the dimension of time.

In summary, the results of my study indicate that even very young children, namely preschoolers, have a rudimentary conception of three-dimensionality which they bring to their work with playdough, which can best be seen in the upright standing figures and the tendency to use the global mass of the playdough rather than flattening it. Further studies will no doubt fill in the gaps in our understanding of the evolution of early three-dimensional concepts. They will clarify the nature of transitional phases and most likely reveal additional spatial concepts that are unique to the three-dimensional medium of clay, Plasticine and Playdough.

References

Arnheim, R. (1974). *Art and Visual Perception: A Psychology of the Creative Eye.* Berkeley, University of California Press.

Brown, E. V. (1975). 'Developmental characteristics of clay figures made by children ages three through age eleven'. *Studies in Art Education*, 16(3): 45–53.

Burt, C. (1921). *Mental and Scholastic Tests*. London, P. S. King & Son.

Burton, J. M. (1981). 'Developing minds: with three dimensions in view'. *School Arts*, 76–80.

Eng, H. (1931). *The Psychology of Children's Drawings*. London, Routledge & Kegan Paul.

Freeman, N. (1980). *Strategies of Representation in Young Children*. London, Academic Press.

Gardner, H. (1980). *Artful Scribbles: The Significance of Children's Drawings*. New York, Basic Books.

Golomb, C. (1972). 'Evolution of the human figure in a three-dimensional medium'. *Developmental Psychology*, 6(3): 385–91.

(1973). 'Children's representation of the human figure: the effects of models, media and instructions'. *Genetic Psychology Monographs*, 87: 197–251.

(1974). *Young Children's Sculpture and Drawing: A Study in Representational Development*. Cambridge, Mass., Harvard University Press.

Goodenough, F. L. (1926). *Measurements of Intelligence by Drawing*. New York, Harcourt, Brace & World.

Grossman, E. (1980). 'Effects of instructional experience in clay modeling skills on modeled human figure representation in preschool children'. *Art Education*, 72(1): 51–9.

Harris, D. B. (1963). *Children's Drawings as Measures of Intellectual Maturity*. New York, Harcourt, Brace & World.

Kerschensteiner, G. (1905). *Die Entwicklung der Zeichnerischen Begabung*. Munich, Gerber.

Leehey, S. C. and Carey, S. (1978). 'Up front: the acquisition of a concept and a word'. Paper presented at the *Tenth Child Language Research Forum*, Stanford, Calif.

Luquet, G. H. (1913). *Les Dessins d'un Enfant*. Paris, Alcan.

    (1927). *Les Dessins Enfantin*. Paris, Alcan.

Martin, H. (1932). 'Die plastische Darstellung der Menschengestalt beim juengeren Schulkinde'. *Zeitschrift fuer Paedagogische Psychologie*, 33: 257–73.

Matz, W. (1912). 'Eine Untersuchung ueber das modelieren sehender Kinder'. *Zeitschrift fuer Angewandte Psychologie*, 6: 1–20.

Piaget, J. and Inhelder, B. (1956). *The Child's Conception of Space*. London, Routledge & Kegan Paul.

Rouma, G. (1912). *Le Language Graphique de l'enfant*. Brussels, Misch. & Thron.

Wilson, M. and Wilson, B. (1982). *Teaching Children to Draw*. Englewood Cliffs, NJ, Prentice-Hall.

Wulff, O. (1932). Kernfragen der Kinderkunst und des allgemeinen Kunstunterrichts der Schule. *Zeitschrift fuer Aesthetik und Allgemeine Kunstwissenschaft*, 26: 46–85.

7
Drama

Gavin Bolton

I am not a psychologist; my interests in drama are primarily educational. What I understand of development in drama is limited to personal observation and to the few attempts that have been made by others to put forward their developmental theories. There has been no serious empirical investigation of the psychology of dramatic development, nor indeed of dramatic activity as a behavioural phenomenon. Among early writers in psychology, Groos (1901) identified its central characteristic of 'dual consciousness', later expressed vividly by Vygotsky: 'the child weeps in play as a patient, but revels as a player' (Vygotsky 1976: 549).

Since the beginning of the century, drama teachers (Harriet Finlay-Johnson, a village school headmistress, was the first to publish [c. 1908] in this country) have claimed that learning is activated by this special state of mind, or 'dual affect', as Vygotsky calls it. Psychologists, including educational psychologists, on the other hand, seem to have shown little interest. The dramatic play of young children has been seen as the province of the clinic rather than of the classroom. Typical of publications combining expertise in both psychology and education is *Imagination and Education* (Egan and Nadaner 1988), which, while acknowledging the value of symbolic play in the preschool child, fails to give credence to an extension of that particular kind of imaginative behaviour in the child of school age.

Even where psychologists have taken an interest in dramatic play, they have only done so in so far as the phenomenon appeared to fit particular theories of mental development. Their conclusions have sometimes been curiously at odds. Whereas, for instance, Vygotsky (1976) claims that young players are at their most mature because they abide by self-imposed rules leading to delayed gratification (he cites the example of the candy which for the duration of the imaginative play remains untouched because of its 'inedible properties'), Piaget explicitly states:

> Unlike objective thought, which seeks to adapt itself to the require-
> ments of external reality, imaginative play is a symbolic transposition
> which subjects things to the child's activity, *without* rules or
> limitations.
>
> (Piaget 1962: 89, my emphasis)

The first British pioneer to attempt a theory of development in drama was
Peter Slade. Influenced by a Froebelian philosophy of child-centreness, he saw
drama as a seed within the child which could flower under the guidance of a
loving parent or teacher into an expressive art. The very title of his seminal
work *Child Drama* (1954) reflects this somewhat romantic view of a child's
capacity for self-expression through art.

As we shall see, the pattern of theoretical thinking set by Slade in respect of
a developmental dimension to children's drama was faithfully followed by a
relatively few pioneers to whom we shall need to give some attention in the
next section of this chapter. Most writers in drama in education (including
this author – Bolton 1979, 1984, 1986) however, have eschewed even modest
attempts at any kind of developmental framework. There are a number of
explanations for this, perhaps the most obvious being that the efforts of Peter
Slade and his followers have not made much impact on the rest of the
profession (in respect of a developmental theory, that is). Their efforts have
not even been challenged; they have just been ignored. There is of course
another kind of explanation. It comes in the form of an admission that our
limited knowledge of what we mean by development in drama makes us both
cautious about criticizing their brave attempts and resolute in our avoidance
of putting forward alternative theories.

Early attempts at a developmental rationale

Slade's attempt to draw up a developmental scheme was a reaction to a
popular view held in the 1940s and into the 1950s that stage acting was a
good thing for children of all ages. He wanted to draw the attention of parents
and teachers to the harm that can be done to children's natural ability when
they are put in front of an audience to show their 'rehearsed piece'. With this
purpose in mind Slade evolved a developmental framework which introduced
the notion of performance readiness.

He claimed that the beginnings of drama can be detected from babyhood
and that the child's experiments in movement, sound and rhythm represent
the earliest stages of music, drama and dance. He draws an important
distinction between what he calls 'personal' and 'projected' play (Slade 1954:
29). 'Personal' play involves the whole person (body and mind) as in running,
jumping and impersonating, whereas 'projected' play does not use the body
but applies the mind to something outside the self – to toys, models, drawing,
writing, and so on. Whereas personal play leads eventually to adult acting,
projected play leads to directing in the theatre. Slade pays most attention to

the former in his publications, and offers a theory of progression of personal play.

He claims that the social development of children is marked by a tendency to group themselves in identifiable spatial shapes in their natural play. The close circle, so important to the under-5, becomes a running circle or spiral shape with 5 to 7 year olds, with its members equidistant from each other. From 7 to 12 the preference is for small 'gang' circles, and from 12 to 14 children naturally seek different levels so that there can be a tongue-shape flow on and off a stage. Eventually, at adolescence, they are ready for the proscenium arch where their acting for the first time will be uni-directional towards an audience instead of the more natural 'acting-in-the-round'.

Brian Way (1967), a contemporary of Slade but publishing a decade or so later, pursued the notion of drama for personal development parti-cularly in respect of what he saw as 'facets of personality': the senses; imagination; physical self; speech; emotion; intellect and concentration. This curious list provided the basis for a programme of developmental exercises involving direct experiences, story-making, improvisation and play-making. Most items on the list each take up a chapter in which a series of progressive exercises ranging from infant to secondary schooling are recommended.

Over twenty years later the contents of this book seem heretical to drama teachers in this country, and yet Brian Way, a charismatic figure, had an overwhelming influence in the 1960s, particularly on some British teacher-training institutions where a generation of students proceeded to perpetuate the myth that developing the senses and the imagination through a shopping-list of graded exercises was what drama education was about. His book has been sold world-wide and has been translated into more languages than any other drama education publication. Currently it is a teacher-training text in Japan, and in Canada, where creative drama in the 1970s was called *developmental drama* out of respect for Way's philosophy and methods. Even today drama publications in certain states of Canada include his book as a highly recommended text. Although this is not the case in curriculum docu-ments in the UK, it nevertheless further explains why those of us who have attempted alternative theories of drama in education, have been reluctant, with memories of false trails still relatively fresh, to commit ourselves to a rationale of development.

Richard Courtney whose first book, *Play, Drama and Thought* (1968), clearly placed him as a disciple of Slade and Way but with an interest in broadening our theoretical understanding of drama by drawing on academic material from other disciplines, has continually given his professional atten-tion (he has spent most of his career with Canadian universities) to issues related to development in drama. But whereas his predecessors' theories of development may seem simplistic and naïve, Courtney's, by contrast, are so intertwined with psychological, sociological, aesthetic, moral and linguistic strands that one can easily be overwhelmed by the complexity of the subject-matter.

In his more recent book *The Dramatic Curriculum* (1980), Courtney outlines a number of academic base-lines from which he builds a coherent framework of what he calls dramatic age stages (pp. 39–60). (He also engages with the sequential development of the dramatic process itself in a way that is informative but not so relevant here.) He is conscious that with so much work done on mental development by renowned theorists such as Piaget, Erikson, Kelly, Bruner and Kohlberg, any theory of personal growth through drama must draw on their combined received wisdom. In other words, if drama has the capacity for influencing the maturing process of a child, then the observer must be alert to the possibility that any such change allegedly brought about by drama might fall into any one or more of the following categories: cognitive; affective; psycho-motor; moral; social; linguistic; aesthetic; role identification; personality traits; and a sense of theatre. Courtney courageously brings all these together and provides us with the following *dramatic age stages*:

1. The Identification Stage (0–10 months)
2. The Impersonation Stage – 'the Child as Actor' (10 months to 7 years)
   (a) The Primal Act (10 months)
   (b) Symbolic Play (1–2 years)
   (c) Sequential Play (2–3 years)
   (d) Exploratory Play (3–4 years)
   (e) Expansive Play (4–5 years)
   (f) Flexible Play (5–7 years)
3. The Group Drama Stage – 'The Child as Planner' (7–12 years)
4. The Role Stage – 'The Student as Communicator' (12–18 years)
   (a) Role 'appearance' (12–15 years)
   (b) Role 'truth' (15–18 years)
   In each case, a later stage has within it each of the previous stages. That is, the adolescent as communicator is at the same time an actor and a planner, and constantly needs to revert to these earlier roles.

Courtney then proceeds to detail, drawing on developmental tables of various authoritative writers, the kinds of behaviours (cognitive, moral, dramatic, etc.) that he claims are most likely to be observed in children doing drama at each age phase. But whereas this appears to be a theoretical advance, the illustrations of children's drama which are supposed to demonstrate the validity of this developmental framework bear very little relationship to contemporary drama in British schools. Now I am not sure whether this discredits Courtney's theories, discredits the drama he practises or discredits the work we do in the UK!

That aside, a perhaps even more telling issue is raised. If any attempt to evolve a developmental framework for drama necessitates taking cognizance of all these aspects of human behaviour, any attempt to record progress will be so absurdly selective and reductive as to be pointless. One might as well pose the question, 'What does *education* do for the maturing process?' – or even 'What is the developmental framework for *life*?'

Theories of art education

In the last ten years or so arts educators in the UK have been encouraged as a matter of political expediency to see their individual specialisms as parts of a total arts experience. From the government point of view, allocating a percentage of curriculum time to *the arts* is a way of appearing to support this aspect of education while actually reducing the amount of time to each subject or even excluding some subjects, such as drama. (In the UK the current Education Reform Act (1988) includes music and art as the only arts subjects in the new 'national curriculum'.) From headteachers' point of view having one subject area makes timetabling seem more manageable, and some teachers feel that uniting the various specialists under the same subject umbrella gives them more political clout.

In this political climate attempts by some writers in the last ten years or so to outline theories of art education have been seen as timely. Perhaps the most influential of these attempts have been made by Robert Witkin (1974) and Malcolm Ross (1978), who, in building on the work of Jean Piaget and Arnaud Reid have created a sophisticated rationale based on the assumption that psychological processes can be identified which are common to all the arts. They argue that these processes should provide the base-line from which all teachers should work irrespective of their specialism.

Malcolm Ross, in particular, makes a stab at developmental programmes, and although he includes illustrations of drama teaching to underpin these, the illustrations are all drawn from his work with adults; this makes it difficult for the reader to envisage what Ross's developmental framework in drama might look like. Similarly, the Gulbenkian Foundation's national enquiry report *The Arts in Schools* (1982) eschews a developmental perspective and fails to give any attention to non-performance drama. The Assessment of Performance Unit of the Department of Education and Science document, *Aesthetic Development* (1983), confines its attention to dimensions of assessment but fails to offer a developmental perspective. David Aspin (1986), another philospher/educationalist who writes frequently about arts education, neither attempts a developmental schema nor makes reference to the practice of classroom drama. It is not merely the case that these writers neglect developmental issues as well as drama, serious as these omissions are, but it is rather that one senses a very narrow view of drama when they do refer to it. None of them appear to read publications on drama education (a glance at their bibliographies is evidence enough), so that they may well not be aware of current theory and practice in the field. (Peter Abbs's book, *Living Powers* [1987], it should be noted, is an exception in this regard.) The only author writing on arts education generally whose theories appear genuinely to embrace a broad practice in drama is David Best (1985). Although he is a philosopher and educationalist of some considerable standing, it is noticeable that his books are also marked by their absence from the above authors' bibliographies. (The art education world is a queer one!) No doubt it is Best's thesis that the purpose of the arts is to do with understanding the world we live in that attracts drama specialists. They feel that this is a view with which they can identify. He makes the following point:

> The peculiar force of learning from a work of art consists in an emotional experience which casts a new light on a situation, revealing what the analogous life situation amounts to.
>
> (Best 1985: 184)

They would claim, I think, that if this is true of the arts generally, then it is even more true of drama; that a kind of responsibility for learning more about the world must *necessarily* accompany the practice of drama in education.

We need now to take a closer look at what I have referred to as present practice. Up to this point in the chapter, I have been concerned to present a picture of what has been done so far in the area of development in drama. The picture is a grim one. Writers fall into two broad categories: those authors who choose to theorize about arts education generally and fail to acknowledge in any substantial way the existence of classroom drama; and those drama specialists who offer developmental theories which seem to have little relevance for current practice. A third category which falls outside the province of the previous two, and which is by far the largest, consists of established authors in the field of drama education who have not yet applied themselves in writing to a developmental scheme. A list of such contributors to the field includes John Allen (1979), Ken Byron (1986), Chris Day (1975), David Davis (1986), John Fines (1974), Dorothy Heathcote (1980; see also Wagner 1979; O'Neill and Johnson 1984), Norah Morgan and J. Saxton (1987), Jonothan Neelands (1984), John Nixon (1987), John Norman and C. Day (1984), Cecily O'Neill and A. Lambert (1982), John O'Toole and B. Haseman (1987), Tom Stabler (1979), Ray Verriour (1985), Margaret Wootton (1982). As I intimated earlier, this chapter will attempt to map out new territory, namely a developmental framework which is derived from a particular philosophy relating drama education to learning. In order to do this, it will be necessary to proceed as follows:

1. To establish what is meant by 'drama as a medium for learning'.
2. To offer my own model of dramatic behaviour. Three distinct modes of behaviour will be identified, only one of which will be seen as relevant to all ages of school children. This one mode, 'dramatic playing', will be described in some detail, as it will serve as a basis for a developmental framework.
3. To further select *one* learning outcome of dramatic playing, namely 'learning to use dramatic form' for consideration in developmental terms.

Drama and learning

The linking of the two concepts in the title by the compilers of *Learning Through Drama: Schools Council Project (Secondary)* (McGregor, Tate and

Robinson 1977), reflected mainstream practice in schools in the UK and set the seal of approval on the movement relating drama to learning which was started by Dorothy Heathcote some twenty years earlier. I would like here to state as succinctly as I can the factors which appear to contribute to the power of drama as a medium for learning.

The claim made by most writers supporting this idea is that drama enhances the *quality* of the learning outcome. Following Piaget's model of development it has been accepted by many educationalists that the acquisition of knowledge (including skills) involves a cumulative process of assimilation and accommodation, the gradual integration of the new with a person's own frame of reference and value system. Extending Piaget's metaphor further one could say that what is learnt becomes 'part of oneself': something understood implies *ownership* of that knowledge. Regrettably much teaching in our schools never gets beyond 'telling' our pupils 'about' the content of what is to be learnt, so that the knowledge remains the 'property' of the teacher. It appears that drama can create the conditions whereby the process of ownership by the learner can be accelerated.

The explanations for this seem to lie in the peculiar socio-psychological structure of the medium of drama. First, the participants adopt an 'as-if' mental set, an imaginative frame of mind giving concrete expression to a hypothetical mode of thinking so that, for example, instead of being required to respond to a teacher's question, 'What would Florence Nightingale's nurses feel when they were refused permission by the doctors to work on the hospital wards at Scutari?', the pupils *are* the nurses and respond *in context*. Second, the learning is necessarily at a level of subsidiary awareness (Polanyi 1958). The teacher may intend to teach, but the pupils do not intend to learn: the intention of the pupils is to create drama. Third, both the drama and the learning are wrought out of group interaction. Fourth, the activity is more independent than is normally possible from the 'hidden curriculum' of teacher power, although, as we shall see, teacher mediation is often of a special kind. Finally, the meanings of words and actions are open to symbolic interpretations.

The combination of these five characteristics gives drama its special dynamic which can release in the participants a high level of energy and motivation, and, more importantly, a capacity for taking themselves along the road of ownership of knowledge. Put another way, we may use a distinction drawn by Guy Claxton (1984) between 'grasping' and 'getting'. The former is more of an intellectual step in the acquisition of knowledge. The latter, however, he describes in the following terms:

Getting is what happens when we understand something in such a way that it has a personal, experiential significance for us ... Instead of being solely an intellectual matter the whole person in both their thinking and feeling aspects becomes involved.

(Claxton 1984: 93)

The quality of learning in drama seems to be of this order.

Drama orientations

We are now ready to take account of the broad categories of drama experience which lead to the above kind of learning. Arts education writers seem to be in broad agreement that three orientations are identifiable, namely forming; performing; and perceiving/reflecting functions, but this distinction may not be so useful if we are looking for a developmental model. Apart from Courtney's account, described earlier, the only attempt in drama that I have come across is offered by John Seely (1976). He sees the young child (below adolescence) involved in an imitative behaviour that is exploratory and calls this *the exploratory model*. The young adolescent is interested in interpersonal behaviours and uses acting techniques to demonstrate his/her ideas to fellow pupils. Seely calls this *the illustrative model*. Finally, Seely terms the public presentation of social ideas through a Brechtian-type theatre *the expressive model*. This model, he suggests, appeals to relatively fewer pupils.

Seely's particular developmental model has some resemblance to my own. Indeed, I will retain the concept of *illustrating* for phase two, but will refer to the first phase as *dramatic playing* and the final phase as *performing a play*. It will be seen that whereas Seely sees each of the orientations as different forms of imitation, I will be at pains to establish that dramatic playing, at its best, is characterized by an independence from imitation.

My own developmental model can be summarized in three phases, and is represented diagrammatically as in Figure 7.1. This diagram represents the whole spectrum of dramatic behaviour: we will consider each of its three modes in turn.

Dramatic playing

The three phases in Figure 7.1 represent a continuum of dramatic behaviour related to the participants' *intention*. It is necessary to identify first the quality of the intention involved in dramatic playing, for the other two categories are characterized by the extent to which they differ from the first. Using an ethnomethodological perspective (so persuasively applied to children's drama by Peter Millward [1988] in his doctoral thesis), it can be said that the participant in dramatic playing has the intention of *managing* a social event, albeit, as he is fully aware, a fictitious one. The behavioural resources he brings to the drama are those he brings to other events in his life, the difference being that some dramas may require managing skills which he is not normally used to drawing upon – for instance, a leadership function, a position of authority, a special language or a special routine. Nevertheless, he draws upon them to the best of his ability in order to create (along with others) the agreed social context and to work spontaneously within it. The essential feeling characterizing the dramatic event is, 'It is happening *now* and we are making it happen.' It is an existential experience.

The quality of spontaneity is often not instantaneously achieved: there are usually a few tentative, awkward and even embarrassing moments (lasting

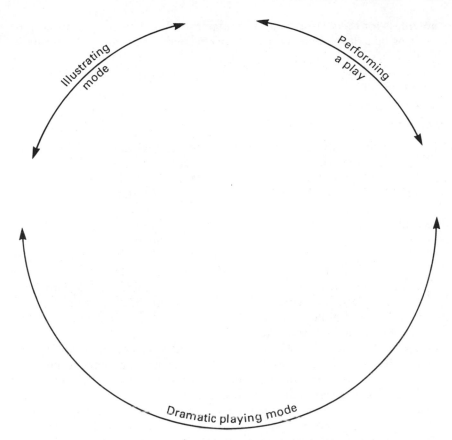

Figure 7.1   Developmental model of children's dramatic behaviour.

seconds/minutes – the longer the 'breaking-in' stage, the greater the feeling of inadequacy), when the creation of the fictitious social context is entirely dependent on a model of that context which the participants proceed to copy. For example, children doing a drama about 'cowboys' will inevitably, in the first instance, engage in *modelling* behaviour until they feel secure enough to be free of it and engage in *managing* behaviour. A vestige of modelling behaviour is retained, but it serves rather than controls the process.

This kind of dramatic activity will be observed in all ages of school children, but age will affect the proportion of time devoted to it. The following percentages, based on my experience, are a rough guide.

Ages 4–9	95%
Ages 10–13	70%
Ages 14+	10%

It can be seen that in spite of the considerable drop in its occurrence at 14+, dramatic playing represents the major mode in the school curriculum as a whole. It is for this reason that the final part of this chapter will concentrate on setting up a developmental framework related specifically to the dramatic playing mode, but it is nevertheless important, in order to give the reader a full picture of dramatic behaviour, to continue here with a brief description of 'illustrating' and 'performing a play'.

Illustrating

Now in the illustrating mode there are three factors which change the nature of the dramatic experience as completely as water into ice. First, the activity is based almost entirely on modelling behaviour. Second, communicability becomes a major criterion of effectiveness and, third, the spectators (fellow class members) take on a responsibility for interpreting, manipulating or directing the players. (Another way of putting this third factor is to say that *percipience* becomes at least as important as participation – this applies even when there is no audience to a group's work, when its members look at what they are doing with an 'outside eye'.) Many different kinds of activity come under this category, from the kind of work introduced by Augusto Boal (1979) and others, involving sculpting and forum theatre, to the psycho-drama and sociodrama of Moreno (1964). A good deal of 'exercise' drama may also be included in this category.

In addition to the three characteristics of modelling, communicability and percipience, other factors may be identified. 'Illustrating' tends to be task-oriented, and short-term, with a strong sense of purpose to do with exploring, demonstrating and responding to ideas about personal and social relationships, and it tends to move imperceptibly into the dramatic playing mode should the sense of 'here and now' take over. For young and older adolescents it offers a rich seam for learning. It is also worth noting here that the teacher's function in the illustrating mode tends to be that of a sensitive chairperson.

Performing a play

This is obviously a more sophisticated and more complex orientation towards performing than 'illustrating'. For instance, the 'given' is hugely expanded: the 'world out there' to be modelled now includes an author's conceptions of themes, context, plot and characterization revealed through dialogue and stage instructions. It may take many weeks of rehearsal before actors feel they 'own' their roles – as opposed to having them 'on loan', as in the illustrating mode.

As they help each other towards 'ownership' during rehearsals, moments of existential behaviour may be sparked off by sudden unexpected changes in the quality of actor to actor interaction, thus temporarily breaking the modelling behaviour. Communicability becomes a top priority so that in addition to 'a world out there' to be absorbed by the actors during rehearsals, they bear in mind an imaginary 'audience out there', which has to be wooed into believing that the 'characters' are 'managing' their own lives. Magic moments in performance can occur when the presence of a responding audience helps the actors feel 'it is really happening'; when their involvement, at least briefly, has the spontaneous quality of dramatic playing and indeed the mode of behaviour has come full circle. These moments may be rare, for in rehearsal the actors have also had to prepare themselves in techniques militating against spontaneity in favour of *repeatability*, a critical factor in defining 'performing a play', for the actors' artifice lies in making the event appear new to audiences night after night.

A few talented pupils in a school with a play production tradition achieve moments of spontaneous dramatic playing arising from a scripted play performance whilst at the same time retaining those techniques aimed at communicability and repeatability. But my guess is that this is a minority group. Much more accessible to most senior pupils is the creation of their own dramatic material which has evolved from a mixture of dramatic playing and illustrating – and which is followed by rehearsing and polishing. In this kind of activity the 'given' of someone else's ideas, dialogue and characterization virtually disappears and most of the techniques (with the exception of achieving repeatability) required of the participants are those practised in the illustrating mode.

Dimensions of a developmental framework in respect of learning to use drama form

Byron suggests that there are three kinds of learning in drama:

1. *Cognitive learning*: (a) development of concepts through the content of the drama or (b) development of cognitive skills, such as hypothesizing, recognizing implications, etc. . . .
2. *Social learning*: development through the social process of drama of the students' capacities to work together productively.
3. *Learning how to use drama form.*

(Byron 1986: 55)

If we attempt to draw up a developmental framework for (1) and (2) we will finish up in the whirlpool of concepts in which, as explained above, Courtney well-nigh drowned himself. We are left therefore with (3), and indeed this writing will focus on *Learning how to use drama form*. But (3) is not independent of (1) and (2); rather (2) and (3) emanate from (1).

I will now discuss in turn each of the five dimensions which, I suggest, are critical to the effective use of form when children are involved in the dramatic playing mode.

Engaging with make-believe

Sara Smilanski (1968) discovered that the children of certain ethnic groups living in Israel were incapable of entering make-believe, which suggests that the existence of what might be called make-believe readiness may be determined by environmental influences. Most children in the Western world achieve a capacity for make-believe play well before school age, but occasionally one comes across some kind of disability in this respect. A distinction needs to be drawn of course between an *incapacity* for make-believe, implying a serious form of maladjustment, and a *disinclination* which may take many forms not necessarily related to age. The experience of starting school may be upsetting and confusing so that an invitation to pretend may simply add to the confusion. No children can enter a make-believe in a context in which they already feel insecure. This particularly applies to adolescents who see drama as 'exposing'. A further cause of inhibition lies in the numbers of participants. The larger the group the more difficult it is to devise and sustain a make-believe experience. There is always a tacitly agreed contract which is more difficult to achieve as the numbers involved grow. This of course has implications for school drama where the numbers in a class tend to average twenty.

Managing skills

I argued earlier that the behavioural skills of drama are not markedly different from those required of any new social situation to which one adapts one's behaviour appropriately. Interestingly, a Department of Education and Science document, *English from 5–16* (1984), in attempting to draw up goals of achievement in English, provides us with most of the criteria we are looking for in respect of 'managing skills' in drama, that is those skills required to initiate and cope with social situations. I list some of the objectives below for the 7-year-olds' group. The authors of course did not have drama in mind, but because the required behaviour is exactly the same, I have added 'in a fictitious situation' in order to reinforce my point.

At the age of 7 most children should be able to:

- Listen to simple instructions and carry them out accurately (in a fictitious situation).
- Comprehend the main idea in simple items of information or explanation given orally (in a fictitious situation).
- Listen actively, so as to be able to ask questions, make comments and respond in other relevant ways to what they have heard (in a fictitious situation).
- Speak sufficiently clearly and audibly to be understood (in a fictitious situation).
- Discuss constructively with other children (in a fictitious situation).
- Ask relevant questions (in a fictitious situation).
- Describe what they have observed (in a fictitious situation).
- Express their feelings to other children (in a fictitious situation).

This list is extended for 11 year olds, so as to include 'make appropriate use of eye contact, gesture, facial expression, pause, tempo and intonation'.

It is interesting that the DES document omits an essential ingredient of social behaviour, that of *identifying the nature of the social situation and the roles required of the participants*. Only with this can the participants carry out the behaviours from the above list. Of course, in drama the logic of the situation may require the participants to adapt to all kinds of distorted social behaviours – they may be required to treat friends as 'enemies'; they may be required to pretend they don't know something; they may have to pretend that they are frightening to other people; they may have to behave as if they are afraid of something; they may have to pretend that they are hungry – just after a heavy school dinner! Whatever the context is, they must recognize its parameters and behave logically within them. This does not mean they should 'put on an act' of being hungry or being afraid: they *are* hungry or they *are* afraid and they set about objectives appropriate to the situation. (Unfortunately, some parents and teachers who misunderstand the nature of dramatic behaviour applaud such a 'show' of emotional states and inadvertently train young children that make-believe requires a superficial form of demonstration.) Even some researchers have fallen into this particular trap as evidenced by the CEMREL project, a report of which was included in *Beyond the Numbers Game* (1972). The following extract is enough to give a flavour of the observers' expectations.

> The teacher gave simple instructions to 'listen, watch arms, body etc.'
> The first three children were sad, happy and surprised in turn. The sad
> girl rubbed her eyes, commenting, 'Oh, I'm so sad'; the happy boy
> jumped up and down and commented, 'Oh I'm so happy; the sun is out.'
> Later anger and fright entered the parade.
>
> (CEMREL Report 1972: 318)

The evaluation included the following kind of judgement: 'Some of the boys as well as the girls were quite stiff and unable to use their bodies to *convey and represent the emotions being expressed*' (my emphasis).

'Reading' teacher-in-role

We need now to give attention to a key aspect of dramatic playing not hitherto mentioned: the responsibility of the teacher. Just as few teachers are likely to say to a class of 20–30 pupils, 'Go on, have a good discussion' and then abandon them, so the teacher needs to be at the helm when leading a drama experience. Dorothy Heathcote (1980) pioneered the technique of teacher-in-role which provides the catalyst for most classroom drama activity. Just as the effective discussion leader guides, draws out, refocuses and challenges, so the drama teacher takes a similar responsibility by playing a part in what is being created. But this responsibility extends beyond that of a discussion leader for drama is an art form, and the teacher works as an artist by elevating the natural managing behaviour of the pupils to a level of selectivity, tension and symbolic resonance which exists beyond their managing skills.

I am making an important distinction here between applying managing skills to the fictitious situation of, say, a 'prisoner-of-war camp' in a way that has sufficient coherence for the activity to be labelled dramatic playing, and the introduction of an artistic (theatrical) dimension into its inner structure which raises the level of dramatic playing to an art form. It is still in the mode of dramatic playing, but 'prisoner-of-war camp' has now taken on a new dramatic intensity and resonates meanings beyond the social context. It has, however limited in scope, some of the qualities of a good play. (Peter Millward's [1988] thesis is pertinent here.) For instance, supposing the 'prisoners' (the pupils) are waiting to signal that the guard has gone off duty so that others can make their escape: the teacher, in role as 'the guard', can use his sense of theatre combined with his understanding of the maturity level of his pupils to build tension in the drama accordingly. With his 9 year olds, he may simply allow their obvious concern to be rid of him to rouse his suspicions; with his 10 year olds he may decide to stay and join them in their card game; with his 13 year olds he may relax and share with them his secret that this is his last day at work and in the process of unburdening ask about their families, talk about his and expound on how there has to be trust between prisoner and warder, that both are victims of a system, and so on. The teacher will select which of these is appropriate, and will be sensitive to the limits of tension that the group can cope with.

I hope this simple example serves to establish that the ability of the pupils in drama is not only dependent on a capacity for imagining a fictitious situation, but also on a set of skills to do with 'reading' and responding to teacher-in-role. A very interesting experiment was conducted recently by Leicestershire teachers. In the report on this, Byron (1987) described how each of four different age groups was given the same dramatic stimulus, and their response recorded. Each class was shown two chairs by which was an old coat and a battered suitcase. Having been asked what 'meanings' they read in this cluster of objects, they were then introduced to teacher-in-role as someone impatiently walking up and down by the side of the objects. After responding to this they were then required, in small groups, to construct their own drama related to what they had seen. Two important findings emerged: the younger pupils tended to 'read' the scene literally, whereas the older pupils introduced symbolic meanings and psychological interpretations. (There is a parallel to this experiment in the work of Bruner [1971: 103–4] who comments on the different levels of meaning with which children engage with comic strips.) Byron also reports that the younger children found it difficult to 'hold onto' the original stimulus once they started to create their own work.

What is missing in this experiment, of course, is the interaction between pupils and teacher-in-role that normally takes place, and which can itself affect their response to the original stimulus. As pupils experience the objects and teacher's role behaviour *in context*, then there is a chance that even for the youngest children it will take on symbolic meanings at, admittedly, a less than conscious level. Nevertheless, the working of the subconscious is paramount in dramatic playing. Young children are unlikely to be able to articulate the symbolic meanings that accrue as the experience proceeds, but it is those meanings above all others that will give the drama its significance.

There is another kind of unconscious learning which takes place. As the teacher, through the use of role, shapes the pupils' 'managing' behaviour in accordance with theatrical form, the pupils gradually develop a sense of what is dramatic, so they too come to appreciate the deliberate formal use of time and space, of contrast, tension, symbolism, ambiguity, contradiction, ritual, simplicity, anticipation, resolution, of completeness and incompleteness, surprise, humour and of magic. It is not enough to impose these as rules of theatre on children when they are older – they need from an early age to feel their significance 'in their bones'. This is *not*, I hasten to say, to be confused with helping children to create a 'good plot', which many teachers have overemphasized in the past; plot is the least important part of dramatic structure.

Under the heading 'Engaging with make-believe' I made the point that the ability of pupils to engage with and sustain make-believe declines in direct proportion to the size of the group. When the teacher takes a role she also takes responsibility for group cohesion as, initially, the pupils become united as *audience* to the teacher's performance. We have seen above that one developmental aspect of the pupils' response is the extent to which they 'read' the teacher's input literally and symbolically. Another aspect of development lies in the ability of the pupils to separate the teacher from his/her normal role, that is the extent to which the normal hidden curriculum of teacher power is overridden by the demands of the fictitious context. Adolescents unused to teacher-in-role will be less skilled than 6 year olds used to drama in this respect.

Sensing what is dramatic

It is one thing to respond intuitively to the teacher's symbolic input; it is quite another to *initiate* behaviours that enhance the drama. One of the first things children have to learn in this respect is delayed gratification (as noted by Vygotsky in his 'poisoned chocolate' anecdote). A child who can just about cope with not eating the candy in play with one other child may find the restraint impossible when shared with six others. And in a whole class situation a teacher is often faced with the child who appears to be a 'spoil sport', breaking the rules of the game, because the self-discipline of delaying is too much.

The tension of waiting is perhaps the first aspect of dramatic form that every child has to learn, and perhaps the second is the power of ritualistic action and words. Linked with these is an understanding that the special use of *space* enhances meaning – for example, the journey, the circle, opposite sides of a threshold, elevation and so on. I believe that young children are capable of initiating these formal elements if the ground has been carefully prepared at a subconscious level by the teacher's use of role. The more sophisticated elements (listed above) may take years to acquire. To understand what is meant by development in drama we certainly need to be able to recognize this particular growth in the child. It is the key to dramatic ability.

Honest reflection

This is the most important part of the learning process, for experience alone means nothing unless the participants reflect with integrity on what has happened in the drama. This in turn feeds back into subsequent drama. The form of the reflection can vary – it may be a class 'discussion', although that is too formal a word for what should be spontaneous sharing of thoughts and, particularly, feelings. Other art forms may be employed – art, poetry, narrative and so on. Often an observer can assess the extent to which the drama has been significant from the quality of this reliving process.

Dramatic playing mode: a summary

In attempting to answer the question, 'Are these children capable of handling the dramatic playing mode?' many of the points made under the above headings relating to the five critical dimensions will need to be considered. A useful way of summarizing is to offer a list of 'profile' questions which might act as a guide to 'where a child is at' in the ability to share a dramatic playing experience with a class of peers and a teacher:

1. Can the child make-believe, that is use objects and actions to represent something not present?
2. Can the child *share* make-believe (a) with another child, (b) in a small group, (c) in a large group? Can the child identify what behaviour is logically required by the fictitious context?
3. Is the child capable of implementing (by managing) that behaviour with appropriate language and actions (a) when it closely coincides with a customary behaviour pattern, (b) when it requires an unusual pattern of behaviour? How inventive is the child in this managing situation – a follower or a leader?
4. Can the child 'read' teacher's role (a) literally, (b) symbolically?
5. Can the child sustain the dramatic significance injected by the teacher? For instance, can the child appreciate and contribute to dramatic tension? Can the child appreciate and sustain the sharpness of the chosen focus?
6. Can the child initiate dramatic elements? Both in planning and in action can the child appreciate what will be effective dramatically?
7. Can the child reflect with sincerity on the nature of the experience? Can the child articulate feelings and thoughts?

The illustrating mode of drama

It is not my intention here to elaborate a detailed model. As indicated earlier I see the focus of this chapter as an attempt to isolate the principal dimensions of the dramatic playing mode, the form of drama which provides the basis for all school drama, but one way of highlighting the principles underlining dramatic playing may be to reiterate, albeit in summary form, the principal features of the illustrating mode, a dramatic orientation of immense educational value to older children.

The illustrating mode can be described as a mirror image of dramatic playing. Whereas the latter has to *feel* right to the participants, the former has to *look* right to the percipients. An 'outside eye' is employed and ability is dependent on how discerning the 'eye' is. There is a strong parallel here with the painter; instead of paints, the medium is people and objects in three-dimensional space. Both 'illustrators' need to be sensitive to form in the use of spatial relationships, texture and colour. For the theatre artist there are usually the added dimensions of time and sound. The prime concern of the participants/percipients is communication to real or hypothetical spectators to whom ideas are to be demonstrated. Thinking centres round obtaining instant effects, and as a result, the formal elements of theatre, often operating at a subconscious level in dramatic playing, become explicit. Members of the group are at pains to articulate to each other about the most effective use (for instance) of grouping. (Even the exercises described in the American CEM-REL project described earlier with their emphasis on 'portraying emotion' have a modest place here, although it should be noted that children of equivalent age in the UK do not usually use this illustrating mode.)

It can be concluded from the above description that 'where the pupils are at' in the illustrating mode of drama is more accessible to observation than in dramatic play. The observer can both hear the public dialogue, where the language of theatre is employed, and can see the immediate results in the action.

It will be obvious to the reader that I have moved away from the traditional assumption that the individual's acting ability is paramount. I believe – and the writings of Ken Robinson (1980) lend support to this view – that it is the audience's/director's sensibilities we should be training in our young adolescents. The skill of an actor belongs to 'performing a play' and is virtually beyond the scope of most school drama.

References

Abbs, P. (ed.) (1987). *Living Powers: The Arts in Education*. London, Falmer Press.
Allen, J. (1979). *Drama in Schools: Its Theory and Practice*. London, Heinemann.
Aspin, D. (1986). 'Objectivity and assessment in the arts: the problem of aesthetic development'. *Inspection and Advice*, 22(1), Summer.
Assessment of Performance Unit (1983). *Aesthetic Development*. London, DES.
Best, D. (1985). *Feeling and Reason in the Arts*. Hemel Hempstead, Allen & Unwin.
Boal, A. (1979). *Theatre of the Oppressed*. London, Pluto Press.
Bolton, G (1979). *Towards a Theory of Drama in Education*. London, Longman.
    (1984). *Drama as Education: An Argument for Putting Drama at the Centre of the Curriculum*. London, Longman.

(1986). *Selected Writings of Gavin Bolton*, edited by D. Davis and C. Lawrence. London, Longman.

Bruner, J. (1971). *The Relevance of Education*. New York, Norton.

Byron, K. (1986). *Drama in the English Classroom*. London, Methuen.

(1987). 'Progression in drama'. An investigation reported by a group of Leicestershire teachers summarized by Byron in *Dance and Drama (2D)*, 7(1), Autumn.

CEMREL Report (1972). 'Extended pilot trials of the aesthetic education program: a qualitative description, analysis and evaluation' (ed. L. M. Smith and S. Shumacher), in D. Hamilton *et al.* (eds.), *Beyond the Numbers Game: a Reader in Educational Evaluation*. Basingstoke, Macmillan.

Claxton, G. (1984). *Live and Learn: An Introduction to the Psychology of Growth and Change in Everyday Life*. London, Harper & Row.

Courtney, R. (1968). *Play, Drama and Thought: The Intellectual Background to Dramatic Education*. London, Cassell.

(1980). *The Dramatic Curriculum*. New York: Drama Book Specialists.

Davis, D. and Lawrence, C. (eds.) (1986). *Selected Writings of Gavin Bolton*. London, Longman.

Day, C. (1975). *Drama for Upper and Middle Schools*. London, Batsford.

DES (1984). *English from 5 to 16*. London, DES.

Egan, K. and Nadaner, D. (eds.) (1988). *Imagination and Education*. Milton Keynes, Open University Press.

Fines, J. and Verrier R. (1974). *The Drama of History*. London, New University Education.

Finlay-Johnson, H. (1920). *The Dramatic Method of Teaching*. London, Nisbet.

Groos, K. (1901). *The Play of Animals*. New York, Appleton Press.

Gulbenkian Report (1982). *The Arts in Schools*. London, Calouste Gulbenkian Foundation.

Heathcote, D. (1980). *Drama as Context*. Sheffield, National Association for Teaching English.

McGregor, L., Tate, M. and Robinson, K. (1977). *Learning Through Drama*. London, Heinemann.

Millward, P. (1988). 'Drama and the medium of language – an ethnomethodological perspective'. Unpublished doctoral thesis, University of Durham.

Moreno, J. L. (1964). *Psychodrama*. New York, Beacon House.

Morgan, N. and Saxton, J. (1987). *Teaching Drama*. London, Hutchinson.

Neelands, J. (1984). *Making Sense of Drama*. London, Heinemann.

Nixon, J. (1987). *Teaching Drama: A Teaching Skills Workbook*. London, Macmillan Education.

Norman, J. and Day, C. (eds.) (1984). *Issues in Educational Drama*. London, Falmer Press.

O'Neill, C. and Johnson, L. (1984). *Dorothy Heathcote: Collected writings on Education and Drama*. London, Hutchinson.

O'Neill, C. and Lambert, A. (1982). *Drama Structures*. London, Hutchinson.

O'Toole, J. and Haseman, B. (1987). *Dramawise: An Introduction to GCSE Drama*. London, Hutchinson.

Piaget, J. (1962). *Play, Dreams and Imitation in Childhood*. London, Routledge & Kegan Paul.

Polanyi, M. (1958). *Personal Knowledge: Towards a Post-critical Philosophy*. London, Routledge & Kegan Paul.

Robinson, K. (1980). *Exploring Theatre and Education*. London, Heinemann.

Ross, M. (1978). *The Creative Arts*. London, Heinemann Educational.
(1984) (ed.). *The Aesthetic Impulse*. Oxford, Pergamon Press.
Seely, J. (1976). *In Context: Language and Drama in the Secondary School*. Oxford, Oxford University Press.
Slade, P. (1954). *Child Drama*. Oxford, Oxford University Press.
Smilanski, S. (1968). *The Effects of Sociodramatic Play on Disadvantaged Pre-school Children*. New York, John Wiley.
Stabler, T. (1979). *Drama in the Primary School*. London, Heinemann.
Verriour, P. (ed.) (1985). 'Face to face: negotiating meaning through drama'. *Theory into Practice*, 24:(3), 181–6.
Vygotsky, L. (1933). 'Play and its role in the mental development of the child', in J. Bruner *et al.* (eds.), *Play: Its Development and Evolution*. Harmondsworth, Penguin, 1976.
Wagner, B. J. (1979). *Dorothy Heathcote: Drama as a Learning Medium*. London, Hutchinson.
Way, B. (1967). *Development through Drama*. London, Longman.
Witkin, R. (1974). *Intelligence of Feeling*. London, Heinemann.
Wootton, M. (ed.) (1982). *New Directions in Drama Teaching*. London, Heinemann.

Part III

Children and the arts
in education

8
Developmental psychology and arts education

David J. Hargreaves, Maurice J. Galton and Susan Robinson

Introduction

Many writers have lamented the gulf that undoubtedly exists between theory and practice in psychology and education. The complaint, often made by theorists as well as practitioners, is that research should be very much more closely allied to the day-to-day concerns of the teacher. This is true in the arts, just as in most other areas of the curriculum. It seems quite likely that the blame for this situation can be laid on both sides. On the one hand, it is almost certainly true that many teachers, for a number of reasons, make little or no attempt to incorporate the results of research into their teaching. This may be because they have no interest in the broader theoretical issues underlying teaching, or it may simply be that they are preoccupied with the pressing demands of running a class.

On the other hand, it is equally true that a great deal of psychological and educational research addresses questions which are of little or no direct concern to the teacher, and there can be a number of reasons for this also. Some kinds of research are easier to do than others; some are more prestigious than others; some are more likely than others to attract funding because of their potential applications, and so on. There are numerous constraints on what can be done in what many see as the relative freedom and luxury of the ivory tower!

To draw a black-and-white distinction between 'theory' and 'practice' is of course to confuse many different shades of grey. There are many different kinds of theorist (in psychology, in educational research and in the arts themselves): different kinds of practitioner (student teachers, class teachers, advisory teachers and headteachers, all of whom have their own perspectives), and the interaction between these groups is increasing, for example on in-service training schemes. The distinction which concerns us most here is that between psychological theorists of child development on the one hand and classroom practitioners on the other.

The contents of this book are clearly rooted in developmental psychology; most of the authors are psychologists. Now although implications for educational practice can potentially be drawn from most of their work, and although most of them would be very likely to express some interest in doing so, the fact remains that this is not their primary aim. Research in developmental psychology has been and to a large extent still is modelled on the natural sciences. Researchers formulate specific hypotheses and carry out experiments to test these hypotheses, often using experimental methodology and quantitative measurement techniques. The result of this approach, as its critics have frequently pointed out, can be an impoverished, short-term and essentially reductionist view of children's learning which is likely to be unrepresentative of the real subtlety and richness of the classroom.

In spite of this, Eisner's (1976) view is that art educators since the 1920s have been more strongly influenced by psychologists' models of development than by those of the educators themselves. He cites the specific influences of Sigmund Freud, Herbert Read and Victor Lowenfeld, in whose work art educators found an invitation 'to unlock the child's creativity and to enable him to express those feelings and images that were stifled in rigid, authoritarian elementary school classrooms' (Eisner 1976: 7), and that this invitation was taken up most readily by followers of the 'progressive movement' in education.

Eisner goes on to suggest that the adoption of this progressive, 'psychological' view in art education had three important practical consequences for pedagogical practice. The first was that teachers were stimulated to look for meanings in children's art which were not necessarily there – to act, probably mistakenly, as untrained amateur psychologists. The second was to encourage teachers to think of themselves more as providers of the appropriate conditions, attitudes and environments for children's art than as didactic directors of class work. Third, and perhaps most benignly, Eisner suggests that the influence of depth psychology was to emphasize to teachers the importance of art in promoting positive mental health and creativity through self-expression, and the development of imagination.

Now whilst this historical view of the relation between psychological theory and pedagogical practice may be perfectly legitimate, it must be pointed out that the psychological models of development were not proposed with education in mind, and indeed several writers have argued that arts education is desperately in need of a specific theoretical framework of its own. Swanwick, for example, argues in the case of music education that research tends to be *under-theoretical*: that it 'drifts aimlessly towards the arbitrary and the irrelevant; lacking principled engagement with the liveliness of intellectual ideas' (Swanwick 1988: 123). Similarly Ross, calling for a coherent theory of aesthetic development, expresses the view that 'Unless curriculum design and assessment are based on a clear conception of development it is difficult to see how either could be the outcome of coherent planning or stand up to public evaluation' (Ross 1982: vii).

We would like to suggest that some of these problems may best be tackled by bringing together workers from each side of the fence between 'theory' and 'practice'. Developmental psychologists have finally begun to recognize that a very incomplete picture emerges when children are studied 'in a vacuum'; their behaviour must be seen in the context of the day-to-day activities of real life. The study of artistic development should be based on activities which are part of the regular curriculum, and which are carried out in the classroom, rather than upon artificial 'tests' which are imported from the psychological laboratory. At the same time the resources and skills of the psychologist, including a wealth of theoretical models and methodological techniques, ought to have quite specific contributions to make to the theory of art education.

In this chapter we chart three areas which are growing parts of the 'middle ground' between psychological theory and educational practice in the arts. We look first at those theoretical developments, largely within psychology, which are currently under way; in particular at the ways in which the theories of Piaget, Gardner, Bruner and Vygotsky can deal with the real-life trans-actions that take place in teaching. We look, second, at those observational studies of classroom practice which address similar questions: these are largely to be found in the educational research literature. The third main area of growth is that concerned with the issue of assessment. The assessment of children's abilities and achievements in the arts poses several unique prob-lems, and it seems likely that these can only be tackled from a multidisciplin-ary viewpoint which encompasses psychological theory as well as class-room practice. The authors' own efforts towards this end in the DELTA (Development of Learning and Teaching in the Arts) project are briefly discussed in this section, and the chapter concludes with a look towards the future.

Learning and teaching in the creative arts

The distinction between *acculturation* (or enculturation) and *training* is very useful in helping us to understand the complementary nature of psychological and educational explanations of child development, and Sloboda (1985) has spelt out the criteria which might be used to determine whether any particular age-related change in behaviour comes into one category or the other. In essence, acculturation refers to those changes which take place spon-taneously, without self-conscious effort or direction. Most children in a given cultural group show a similar sequence of achievements as a result of their common socialization experiences, and the steps of this sequence occur at roughly similar ages. Training, on the other hand, refers to the process of trying to promote specific behavioural changes in a conscious, directive manner.

This is very similar to Gardner's distinction between *unfolding* and *train-ing* in his discussion of teaching in the arts. The 'unfolding' or 'natural' perspective views the child 'as a seed, which, though small and fragile, contains within its husk all necessary "germs" for eventual artistic virtuosity' (Gardner 1976: 99). A strong version of this view, perhaps best exemplified by Piaget's theory, implies that the teacher's role is largely protective, or preventive; her job is to provide the appropriate conditions for those developments which come from *within* the child. The 'training' view, on the other hand, holds that this is not enough: like seedlings, children need special attention and cultivation if they are to develop properly. The influence of this view is seen most clearly in some of the behaviourally oriented classroom techniques which are used in North America (see e.g. Madsen and Yarborough 1980). These place a very strong emphasis on the teacher's control of the learning process.

Gardner points out that it is all too easy to draw this distinction and then sagely to pronounce that the ideal position is somewhere in between; that the teacher's role should be to provide an optimal learning environment *and* to direct children within it. The day-to-day truth of the matter, in British schools at least, is that the diversity of the activities subsumed under 'teaching' genuinely encompasses both approaches. Preliminary data from the authors' DELTA project confirm this point of view: the visual art, writing and musical activities employed by the teachers in our study range from the very directive to the very non-directive, and of course some individual teachers employ activities from both extremes of this scale in conjunction with one another.

Although the distinction may be blurred in practice, it is nevertheless very useful for our purposes to consider the positions of the prominent psychological theories of development in relation to it. It would not be appropriate to expound the theories of Piaget, Gardner, Vygotsky and Bruner at any length here, and we shall make no attempt to do so. What we *shall* try to do is to compare their respective views of the teacher–child relationship in the particular context of the creative arts.

We mentioned earlier that Piaget's theory (see e.g. Boden 1979) adopts a fairly strong form of the 'unfolding' view. For Piaget, the child is a 'mini-scientist' who is internally motivated to explore the world through the process of *equilibration*. The child's thinking is seen to be in the unstable state of disequilibrium in relation to new objects and experiences, and this state is resolved by the assimilation of those objects and experiences. The teacher's role is to promote this process by providing learning experiences which display *optimal discrepancy* between the level of thinking which the child has reached and the level it might potentially reach. Relatively little learning will take place if the activities provided are too easy or too difficult: a moderate level of difficulty is most effective. The most important feature of this view is that the motivation for learning primarily comes from within the child herself rather than from the teacher.

There are numerous well-documented critiques of Piaget's theory (see e.g. Brown and Desforges 1979; Modgil, Modgil and Brown 1983), and two of these bear directly upon our argument. The first is that Piaget pays insufficient attention to the actual cultural context within which learning occurs; that he sees cognitive development as a kind of insatiable mental appetite which consumes all before it, and that similar developmental progressions occur in all children no matter what is consumed. The critics of this view (e.g. Bruner, Olver and Greenfield 1966) argue that much more emphasis should be placed on the nature of what is consumed. In the present context the argument is that the specific activities provided by the teacher, and the prevailing climate within which they are presented, have a much more far-reaching impact than Piagetian theory allows.

The second line of criticism is fundamental to the alternative theory of artistic development proposed by Gardner (1973), which was described in Chapter 1. Gardner sees Piaget's view that children attain increasingly sophisticated forms of scientific thought as being far too narrow since it neglects most of the irrational, non-scientific processes which are involved in the arts. The crux of Gardner's own theory is that the 'concrete operations' and 'formal operations' which Piaget sees as the basis of cognitive development in later childhood and adolescence are not necessary for fully-fledged 'participation in the artistic process'; that by the age of 7 most children have achieved the essential characteristics of the audience member, artist and performer. As we saw, Gardner proposes an informal model of artistic development with just two broad stages, namely a 'presymbolic period' in the first year of life during which different artistic 'symbol systems' unfold and differentiate, and a 'period of symbol use' from ages 2 to 7 in which these symbol systems become enmeshed with the conventions of the culture.

Now this leads us back to the issue of unfolding and training. Gardner suggests that the early years of life, that is those within his period of symbol use, 'constitute a time of natural development of artistic competence' (Gardner 1976: 108). The teacher's task in these years is thus primarily to provide support for those developments which occur naturally: to respond sympathetically to initiatives which come from the child. During middle childhood and later, however, more active intervention is called for: more directive forms of training are appropriate for the learning of specific artistic skills and techniques.

Some developmental theorists would go much further than Gardner in recommending a more directive approach to teaching even at the preschool age. Wood (1987, 1988), for example, argues very convincingly for a conceptualization of the teacher–learner relationship which derives from the theories of Vygotsky and Bruner. Vygotsky (1978) put forward the notion of the 'zone of proximal development', which is the discrepancy which exists between the level of the child's performance on a given task at any given point in time, and her potential level of performance on that task after receiving appropriate instruction. This notion imparts far more importance to the input of the teacher than is present in Piagetian theory. In essence, Vygotsky's theory puts the *capacity to learn from instruction* at the heart of intellectual development.

A second notion which is central to Wood's argument is that of *scaffolding*, which he has developed in conjunction with the work of Bruner (e.g. Wood, Bruner and Ross 1976). Whereas the 'zone of proximal development' specifies the domain within which instruction ought to take place, scaffolding is a metaphor which describes the *process* by which the teacher builds upon the child's existing orientation towards the learning task. Wood and his associates have undertaken a number of experimental studies, notably of mother–child pairs working together on a wooden construction toy task (e.g. Wood and Middleton 1975), which have enabled him to specify five types of scaffolding which manifest varying degrees of teacher (in this case maternal) control. These range from 'general verbal prompts' (representing the lowest level of control), through 'specific verbal instructions', 'indicates materials' and 'prepares for assembly' to 'demonstrates' (highest degree of control). Wood's studies showed that mothers vary widely in their use of these different strategies, and that their 'teaching styles' had a strong influence on the children's learning.

This interdependence of teacher style and pupil learning poses the important question of *contingency*: in an interactive learning situation, who is dependent on whom? Does the pupil take the lead in initiating actions which the teacher then builds upon, or does the initial lead (or 'task induction') come instead from the teacher? The answer seems to be that this depends very much on the nature of the learning task, as well as on the setting in which it occurs. The notion of scaffolding has been applied by Bruner, Wood and others to the analysis of mother–child interactions and language development, that is to activities which are very much less structured than simple problem-solving tasks which have one correct answer.

Wood explains these differing patterns of learning in terms of the important distinction between *natural* (spontaneous) and *contrived* teaching situations. He draws on the work of Tizard and Hughes (1984), amongst others, which clearly demonstrates that children 'present themselves' and generally behave very differently in learning situations at home and at school. In the natural setting of the home, preschoolers are very much more likely to initiate activities, for example to spontaneously ask questions of their caregivers, since these are embedded in the day-to-day business of real life. At school, on the other hand, a good deal of learning is *contrived*. As we shall see in the next section, the control of learning interactions is firmly in the hands of the teacher. Classroom observation studies show that this is just as true in the teaching of arts subjects, which might be thought to involve expressive, open-ended interactions with minimal teacher control, as in any other (Delamont and Galton 1987).

Delamont and Galton's conclusion is based on their *ethnographic* research in the classroom; theirs is one of several studies in arts education collected together by Tickle (1987) which adopt this approach. Let us conclude the present section by looking briefly at a speculative theory of aesthetic learning which derives from the same research tradition, and which thereby takes a different viewpoint from the psychological theories we have discussed so far. David H. Hargreaves (with whom the editor of this book has unfortunately been confused on a number of occasions!) makes the distinction between what he calls 'incremental' and 'traumatic' theories of learning. The former, he argues, are the 'common sense' ideas of learning shared by most teachers: that children gradually accumulate increasingly complex and sophisticated repertoires of skills, knowledge and understandings by a process in which each new acquisition is built upon previous ones.

Hargreaves (1983) regards most of the psychological theories of learning we have discussed so far as falling into this category. He feels that while these may go so far in explaining the *aesthetic* learning which is specific to the arts, they leave some vital and unique aspects of it unexplained. Hargreaves proposes that a *traumatic* theory of aesthetic learning is needed as a complementary part of any comprehensive explanation. This stems from the observation that some informants describe their response to certain art works as disturbing, or even shattering; their normal mental state is somehow unbalanced in these moments, and this has a powerful impact on their learning and long-term memory.

Hargreaves suggests that 'conversive traumatic experiences' such as these possess four elements. There is initially a powerful *concentration of attention*; the perceiver becomes 'lost in' the art object, and the sense of time and space is suspended. This is accompanied by a *sense of revelation*, an emotional reaction 'as if some already existing core of the self is suddenly being touched and brought to life for the first time' (Hargreaves 1983: 141). The third element is *inarticulateness*: the inability to express one's experience in words to others even when the desire to do so is strong. The fourth, and perhaps the most important from the educational point of view, is *arousal of appetite*; the motivation to repeat an experience and to elaborate upon it is an important aspect of that experience.

Hargreaves speculates further about the workings of this fourth element, suggesting that becoming 'hooked' on an art object or art form leads to further commitment and exploration: that exploration increases the observer's discrimination within the domain: and that increased discrimination gives rise to a search for background knowledge in the observer. This proposed causal chain of events is interesting because it reverses the sequence which has commonly been proposed to describe the process of creative *productivity*. The first of Wallas's (1926) well-known theoretical stages of the creative process is *preparation*: background reading and immersion in the subject area is seen as a necessary *prerequisite* of creativity in any given field. Hargreaves seems to be putting this the other way round: his view of aesthetic *perception* is that something like 'retrospective preparation' follows illumination rather than vice versa.

The ultimate usefulness of Hargreaves's theory will probably rest on its testability, and in particular on its capacity to address *causal* questions like that above, as distinct from merely describing some of the salient features of aesthetic learning. We also need to ask whether 'conversive traumatic experiences' only occur in a tiny proportion of people's responses to art objects. It may well be that most people's reactions to art are mundane, routine and 'ordinary' experiences which involve no traumata, emotions or conversions of any kind; some people may indeed *never* respond in this way. At the very least, however, the theory puts an interesting new perspective on 'received views' of artistic learning, and has some novel implications.

Hargreaves sets his theory in the context of the educational distinction between what he calls 'arts lessons' on the one hand and 'art appreciation' on the other. In the former, which are by far the most common, teachers typically help pupils with the production of their own creative art works – and they do so in a relatively non-directive way. The theory of 'traumatic learning' is more likely to throw light on the learning which occurs in 'art appreciation', where the teacher is (maybe rather uncomfortably) involved in the business of instilling standards of artistic taste and style. This distinction raises the question of the 'hidden curriculum' of the classroom: the pupils' view of the lesson as 'doing' or 'listening' almost certainly has a profound influence upon their attitude towards the teacher's contribution, and thereby upon the nature of their learning. Let us look next at some classroom-based research which has been undertaken with this issue specifically in mind.

Classroom processes and artistic learning

In recent years psychologists have become increasingly interested in the study of classroom processes, and this can readily be discerned in the changing contents of textbooks of educational psychology. One standard textbook which ran into seven editions within six years (Lovell 1958) contained no mention of the word 'teaching' in the index of its 1964 edition, for example, whereas a more recent text which is equally well-known (Gage and Berliner 1984) devotes 200 of its 751 pages to the topic. Recent systematic studies of classrooms have been reviewed in the United States by Brophy and Good (1986) and in the UK by Bennett (1987). The research emphasis has now moved away from mere description of 'what happens in the classroom' to a search for a better understanding of the factors which govern the exchanges taking place between teachers and pupils.

In the UK most of these systematic studies have taken place in the primary school, partly because of the concern expressed by politicians and the media about 'modern primary methods' and partly because with one teacher responsible for the whole of the curriculum it is relatively easy to gather a representative sample of data within a limited period of time. Much of the earlier work has served to highlight the gap between the rhetoric and the reality of progressive practice as defined in the Plowden Report (1967), a prominent recommendation of which was that creative activity required strong individualization of the learning process with opportunities for children to work collaboratively so that they could share ideas.

The picture which has emerged from various classroom studies, however, is a very different one (Galton 1987). Teaching in the modern primary classroom is still highly didactic, with the emphasis on giving information and routine instructions rather than on discussion and challenge. The curriculum is often dominated by the so-called 'basic skills', and collaborative group work between pupils in the absence of the teacher is a neglected art.

Primary classrooms remain places where children appear to be heavily dependent on the teacher, and this dependency creates severe problems of organization and management. With one teacher and thirty dependent pupils it is very difficult for the teacher to find enough time to diagnose pupils' learning difficulties so that tasks can be matched to the pupils' needs and abilities. In general, it has been found that children of high ability are set work which underestimates their competence whilst the reverse is true of low achieving pupils (Bennett *et al.* 1984).

Explanations for this and for other features of classroom life are now beginning to emerge. Primary classrooms are places where teachers and pupils bargain with each other to obtain conditions which, as far as possible, satisfy their respective needs. Teachers need co-operation from their pupils (good work and behaviour which demonstrate to parents and to other colleagues that the teacher is competent). Pupils appear to need tasks which can be completed successfully so that they are not seen as failures by the teacher or by their peers. Within this context pupils will quietly complete a simple worksheet, for example, on which they have to fill in missing words from a list written down at the bottom of the sheet; but they may disrupt the class when asked to do more challenging work in which the answers are not so obvious, or not so readily available.

One reason for this bargaining concerns the ambiguity inherent in many tasks which teachers set in the classroom. As Doyle (1979) has pointed out, tasks are not purely academic exercises; they also carry with them behavioural overtones. For example, teachers ask questions not only to find out whether a pupil knows the answer but also to discover whether that pupil is paying attention. The more ambiguous and challenging a question (e.g. one with no correct answer) the more difficult it is for the pupil to know how to respond. Studies of classroom discussion illustrate clearly that in such cases pupils use avoidance strategies so that some other pupil offers an answer. It is then possible from the response to find out what the teacher intended by asking the question (Galton 1987). According to Doyle (1986) academic learning and classroom management are inextricably linked. The more ambiguous the task the higher the risk of failure it carries for pupils and the greater the pupils' attempts to get the teacher to make the task 'safe' either by giving hints about the situation (guided discovery) or by reducing its complexity.

These studies have much to say about the teaching of the creative arts. The writing of poems, the painting of pictures or the creation of pieces of music all involve a high degree of risk-taking on the part of the pupils and present a very difficult situation for the teacher. *Ownership* appears to be an important concept for pupils during such activities, and they may complain bitterly if the teacher 'takes over their idea'. At the same time, however, accepting 'ownership' means that the pupil has to accept the possibility that the audience of teacher and peers may find the work unsatisfying, so that pupil self-esteem is put at considerable risk. One generally accepted 'two-stage' theory of teaching, that by initially giving considerable guidance the teacher helps to build the confidence of pupils so that they gradually begin to experiment more freely, does not seem to be borne out by observational studies (Galton 1987). Indeed the work of Armstrong (1980) and Rowlands (1984) suggests that this approach has the opposite effect and that however problematic for the teacher and for the pupil, it is necessary to allow a period of incubation to take place while the child comes to terms with these twin dilemmas of 'ownership' and 'risk of failure'.

One related difficulty in reducing this ambiguity and thus the risk concerns the pupil's need to understand the teacher's intentions. When setting and monitoring tasks teachers have many purposes often concerned with the needs of individual children. In carrying out a piece of writing, for example, pupils may be told to first discuss an idea amongst themselves, then to write a draft and redraft of these ideas before finally producing a version which can be printed on the class computer and published as part of the classroom display. One pupil may complete a full page, but the teacher may decide that this pupil is capable of further improvement and order a further redraft. Another who has written perhaps only six lines will be encouraged by being allowed to print out what has been written. Children with a reputation for disruption may be similarly rewarded because 'they behaved well and were not silly' during the lesson. Although the teacher may be able to articulate clear reasons for all these decisions it is uncertain whether pupils understand equally well why in some cases a page of writing cannot be published while in other cases six lines can. Asking pupils in such classes 'How do you know when your work is ready to be printed?' may unfortunately elicit a response such as 'I take it to Mr Jones and he tells me'. Such uncertainties add to the risks inherent in creative activities such as story writing.

An important element in the bargaining process and in the removal of risk and ambiguity from creative tasks in the classroom would therefore appear to be the need for teachers to clearly articulate their aims and purposes so that pupils understand what is required of them, and how their ideas and work are being judged. The development of children's art work and their perceptions of teachers' evaluation of it are interdependent: this issue is coming to the fore in the difficult area of assessment, as we shall see next.

Assessment in the arts

For some, the prospect of assessment in the arts is highly undesirable. Ross, for example, vehemently opposes the idea, arguing that the arts have certain unique functions in education. He argues that subjecting the arts to conventional assessment procedures endangers their essential qualities, which include 'imagination', 'freedom', 'fairmindedness', 'passion', 'enchantment', 'musing' and 'sensibility', and that this threatens the concept of a balanced, rounded education. Following his principle of 'arts for all', Ross considers that we should vigorously defend children's right to pursue the arts for pleasure since they are 'intrinsically and self-evidently good' (Ross 1986:

92). As such, they should form part of a 'protected' core of subjects which are outside the bounds of conventional assessment.

Others feel that even given the inclination, we cannot practicably carry out assessment in the arts using the same methods as in other subjects. Aspin (1986) argues that subjects traditionally regarded as having high status (e.g. mathematics and the sciences) gain their respectability because they are seen to be based on 'facts' which are supported by empirical evidence: progress in these subjects is measured by 'objective' methods which derive from positivist traditions. The arts, on the other hand, are perceived as having low status; they are seen as subjects in which evaluation is non-quantifiable, maybe unjustifiable, and prone to individual interpretation and values.

Aspin argues that this division between the 'objective' sciences and the 'subjective' arts is false. In any given subject, appraisal relies on the formulation of a set of criteria which represent the norms or standards of that subject: specific works are judged in relation to those criteria. It follows that the evaluation of a given piece of work is dependent on the extent to which it exhibits the accepted criteria for that specified art domain. For Aspin, these criteria must be established by means of intersubjective agreements amongst people with expert knowledge of the domain, that is those who are familiar with the rules and conventions of the *languages* of different art forms. If a comprehensible and practicable set of criteria can be agreed upon, then 'objective' assessments can indeed be made.

Despite his assertion that the arts *are* objective in this sense, Aspin concedes that the arts and sciences warrant different kinds of objective assessment. Whilst the 'scientific' methods of quantification and verification might be used to assess specific artistic skills, techniques and knowledge, he feels that they are inadequate for measuring equally important skills such as understanding, imagination, sensitivity and insight. It is in these latter areas that Aspin emphasizes the need for common understandings of 'artistic languages': the arts need assessment techniques which are expressed in the terms of particular domains.

Although some authors argue that educators should not assess progress in the arts, and others that they cannot, the plain fact is that they are already doing so. This happens on an individual level; as we have seen, teachers make clear-cut, yet subjective and possibly quite idiosyncratic judgements of their pupils' art work as a routine matter in the classroom. On a national level, assessments of children's artistic progress have been made in North America for many years. In the UK the publication of *The National Curriculum 5–16* (DES 1987a) marks the advent of a new national curriculum and the institution of comprehensive assessments at regular age intervals. This document plainly states the government's intention to establish clear attainment targets and assessment procedures which will enable individual progress to be measured against national standards. The intention is that schools and their headteachers should be more publicly accountable for their work, and that teachers should evaluate children's work more effectively than hitherto.

In the past, teachers have been more familiar with standardized tests than with any other forms of assessment: these have the advantage of being easy to administer and score. They have many well-documented disadvantages, however, which derive from their artificiality; children are assessed 'out of context'. Typically, the standardized test setting is a formal one in which children work on a specific activity within given time limits. Questions or tasks are highly structured and usually unrelated to daily classroom activities. The tests concentrate on specific knowledge and abilities within limited spheres, predominantly the mathematical and the verbal. Children's responses are normally written and timed, and then scaled by reference to predetermined norms. The results, usually in the form of scores, grades, percentiles or rank positions, purport to be objective and relatively stable measures of ability.

These problems apply to standardized assessments in any domain, and the arts clearly present additional problems of their own. The idea of national assessment in the arts is new in the UK, but there may well be lessons to be learnt from the experience of North American educators. In a review of national assessment procedures for the arts in the USA, Gardner and Grunbaum (1986) list over twenty instruments which purport to measure different facets of children's progress. These tests are designed to probe children's production, perception, appreciation and comprehension abilities in the arts; their factual knowledge; their attitudes towards art in general and towards specific works; and their capacity to make value judgements.

Gardner and Grunbaum raise a number of specific criticisms of these instruments, but their most important general point is that this range of tests concentrates on 'linguistic and logical modes of thinking' at the expense of 'artistic thinking'. Gardner's (1983) theory of 'multiple intelligences' implies that competence in one mode of thinking (or 'intelligence') does not necessarily extend to competence in any other, and so the arts have been assessed inappropriately. Gardner and Grunbaum recommend that assessment procedures for the arts should reflect children's progress in mastering the appropriate artistic 'intelligence' (e.g. music, visual art, drama). Their verdict on the American national assessment tests is that these traditional instruments 'have reached their practical limits' in their applicability to the arts.

The ideal alternative to standardized testing would be a workshop environment. Pupils would spontaneously acquire the skills of production, perception and reflection by completing exciting and meaningful projects, guided by charismatic and reflective arts teachers: formal assessment techniques would be replaced by portfolios of work compiled under these conditions (Gardner and Grunbaum 1986). While this might indeed be ideal, it is very unlikely that such an approach to assessment would comply with the current demand for accountability and standardization. On the other hand, as we have seen, current standardized assessment measures do not possess ecological validity. The problem is to find assessment procedures which meet both sets of criteria.

Two initiatives which have attempted to tackle this problem are *Project Spectrum* and *Arts Propel*, both of which are under the auspices of Harvard *Project Zero*. Researchers in both of these projects believe that it *is* possible to merge assessment with daily classroom activities, and their alternative procedures rest on this foundation.

Project Spectrum (Wexler-Sherman, Gardner and Feldman 1988) has developed methods of assessing preschool children in the familiar context of the classroom setting. Semi-structured assessment activities have been devised which are based on everyday classroom apparatus, and which are interesting and attractive to children. For example, musical perception is measured by a Montessori bells task and narrative language by a story-telling board. There is no specific assessment time; instead, the assessment materials are made continuously available on the assumption that each child will become engaged in all activities at some time during the school year. The Project Spectrum assessors, though not classroom teachers, are familiar with the children and interact informally with them. Children's activities are recorded unobtrusively, in the classroom and on the playground, by means of observations and tape recordings. The information collected about each child is used to form a profile which can reveal different patterns of ability between individuals, as well as individual progression and development over time. The Project Spectrum assessment tasks aim to measure a wider range of children's abilities than is covered by traditional tests. They currently include capacities in the spheres of music, number, visual arts, movement, science and language.

The Arts Propel project (Wolf 1988a, 1988b) has initiated arts assessment procedures for the secondary (high school) age range, and publishes a regular newsletter (*Portfolio*) which disseminates these amongst teachers and researchers. The project works from the three basic premises that arts assessments should take qualitative issues into account; that they should examine process as well as product; and that pupils' opinions of their own art works should be taken into account. This leads to a three-tiered approach to appraisal.

First, pupils are presented with a problem-solving *project* which enables teachers to examine their efforts to formulate ideas and to follow them through to the production stage. Second, *portfolios* encompassing several projects allow teachers to study pupils' progress and development over time. Finally, by means of *reflective interviews*, teachers can evaluate how much insight pupils have into their own work. In these interviews pupils appraise the quality of their own projects and portfolios in terms of skill, style, progress, how pieces of work evolved towards the final product, and how they could work on their strengths and weaknesses to improve their future performance.

In the UK, the Report of the National Curriculum Task Group on Assessment and Testing (the Black Report: DES 1987b) has set out initial guidelines for assessment in all areas of the new national curriculum. The report considers that teachers' continual classroom assessments provide a wealth of valuable insight into pupil attainments and abilities, although the problem at the national level is to ensure comparability between individual teacher evaluations. Assuming that the Report's proposals are implemented, this problem will be dealt with by instituting group moderation meetings at which teachers will bring their own assessments into line with national standards. Comparisons will also be made with newly-instituted standardized assessment tasks (tests, practical tasks and observations) which will be provided by external test development agencies.

Very little has been said by the Task Group so far about specific plans for the arts, although it seems reasonable to assume that continuous assessments of ongoing class work, carried out by teachers, will form an important part of the new system. We have seen already that no single method of assessment can be appropriate for the evaluation of educational attainment in all aspects of the arts: different methods of assessment are demanded by different types of activity, their objectives and their expected outcomes. The assessment of specific skills, techniques and knowledge requires different procedures from those best employed in the evaluation of qualities such as insight and imagination. It is in this latter sphere of *qualitative* evaluation where the principal problem for arts assessment lies: how can qualitative measures be made reliable?

According to *Aesthetic Development*, a discussion document produced by the Assessment of Performance Unit of the Department of Education and Science in the UK (DES 1983), the solution to this problem lies in clarifying the criteria for what constitutes artistic achievement. Teachers and pupils will only be able to assess the artistic progress of themselves and others when they have a clear mutual understanding of what constitutes achievement. At present there is no such understanding, and so research is badly needed in this area.

In the authors' view, a set of agreed criteria can only be established if arts teachers are closely consulted. Their role in assessing ongoing work is vital since they alone engage in daily interactions with the children who are to be assessed: teachers are uniquely able to carry out and interpret assessment procedures. Since teachers will themselves have the responsibility of conducting national assessments in the new British scheme, it is of paramount importance that they approve of and validate the new procedures. The success of the procedures will depend on their co-operation and support. Teachers' confidence in and commitment to the new assessment system is likely to be much greater if they have been involved in its formulation.

The authors' DELTA (Development of Learning and Teaching in the Arts) project began in late 1987. Some preliminary findings are outlined here, and full reports of the research will be published in due course. Our primary aim is to investigate how primary school teachers assess children's work in the creative arts on an everyday basis. Initial interviews with sixteen teachers in the Leicestershire area suggest that they have strong implicit notions about what constitutes achievement in music, visual art and writing. Whilst all of these teachers acknowledged that they continually assess children's progress so as to enable them to guide the next stage of learning, most were unable to articulate the criteria on which they base their qualitative evaluations. The implicit knowledge which teachers evidently possess and regularly use in their classrooms needs to be teased out of individuals. Our aim is to make this knowledge explicit, and to establish a consensus of opinion about the criteria which determine quality in children's art work.

As part of their initial interviews, the teachers were asked to describe activities in music, visual art and writing which they had found to be successful with their classes. Repertory grid techniques were next used to generate a set of bipolar constructs which different teachers use in making discriminations between these activities. In this way we have begun to elucidate the implicit criteria which teachers apply to different arts activities. We also plan to obtain systematic evaluations of children's work on these tasks, using similar techniques. These evaluations should enable us to develop a language of arts assessment which is comprehensible to all teachers and which may help to facilitate communication between them.

The establishment of a successful national assessment system relies not only on teachers sharing its aims but also on their ability to use it effectively, reliably and confidently. In the course of our DELTA project interviews several teachers expressed their concern that new assessment procedures might be so time-consuming as to encroach on their ability to get on with the job of teaching. Some also felt that they lacked expertise in assessment: that they were inadequately prepared to assess their pupils' progress. Extensive pre-service and in-service training must be provided to ensure that all teachers feel confident that they have mastery of the skills and techniques which they will need to make reliable and meaningful observations and interpretations. The institution of a national assessment system requires considerable investment not only in terms of additional facilities and resources but also in terms of teacher time and commitment.

Conclusion

Our thesis in this chapter is that psychological researchers and educational practitioners have complementary needs, and that collaboration between them should be of considerable mutual benefit. This applies to all areas of the curriculum, but it may be particularly pronounced in the arts. On the one hand, psychological theories of artistic development are woefully underdeveloped as compared with their scientific counterparts; on the other hand, arts education is clearly urgently in need of a coherent theoretical framework.

We have outlined three main areas in which these aims might be pursued, namely the development and application of psychological theories of teaching and learning; studies of classroom processes; and assessment in the arts. A good deal of the research that we have described reflects the growing trend towards a view of the child as someone who has to 'make sense' of the social world, which carries with it the strong implication that laboratory studies must be complemented by 'naturalistic' research carried out in real-world situations. Bruner and Haste (1987) have recently described the main theoretical features of this trend and have collected together a number of research studies which exemplify it.

Within the field of children's artistic development we could say that there is a general move away from general or *universal* explanations, and towards more specific or *particular* ones. Let us conclude this chapter, and the book as whole, by describing three manifestations of this movement.

In Chapter 1 we saw that studies of creative productivity have begun to move away from the measurement of general characteristics of people and towards the investigation of specific products within a given frame of reference. We also saw that theories of artistic development are moving away from generalized explanations of age-related changes occurring *across* art forms and towards domain-specific explanations *within* art forms. Both of these trends represent the move from the general to the particular from the point of view of developmental theory.

When we turn to theories of teaching and to systematic studies of classroom processes, the trend is away from generalized descriptions of children's progress and teaching styles and towards the investigation of the *meanings* of the interactions that take place. Educational researchers are beginning to get to grips with social psychological questions such as the bargaining and negotiation that takes place between teachers and pupils, and the intellectual ownership of classroom work: they are moving beyond the level of description. This is what Bruner and Haste (1987) mean when they talk about the study of social representations; the focus is on the 'mutual construction of meaning' in the classroom.

Finally, in considering the question of assessment, it is becoming increasingly clear that the traditional psychometric approach, in which the tester makes a detached and objective appraisal of the subject's abilities or progress under standardized conditions, is inadequate in the arts as well as in other areas of the curriculum. Research projects such as Arts Propel and Project Spectrum in the USA and the authors' own DELTA project are beginning to demonstrate that educators should carry out assessment as an integral part of the teaching process. We are beginning to see 'tests' or assessments as part of course work rather than as separate and unrelated activities.

The implication of this is that the contents of assessment procedures will become very much more 'naturalistic' or 'ecologically valid' as far as specific teachers and localities are concerned, and this will lead to their overall diversification from the national point of view. Assessment will involve prior knowledge of pupils on the part of teachers, and perhaps also on the part of pupils themselves. This move clearly implies that the process of assessment is inextricably bound up with children's artistic development. In other words, the concerns of the developmental psychologist, the teacher and the educational assessor cannot be neatly parcelled out from one another.

We need to use all the methodologies and techniques at our disposal in tackling the diversity of this subject area. This encompasses philosophical, sociological and historical analyses, ethnological observation in classrooms, psychometric testing and other forms of assessment, *as well as* more rigorous quasi-experimental investigations, where these are possible. The problems posed by the arts are too diverse, complex and mysterious to be tackled by any single method.

Acknowledgement

The authors would like to acknowledge the support of the Economic and Social Research Council (grant C0023 2418) to the DELTA (Development of Learning and Teaching in the Arts) project, Department of Psychology and School of Education, University of Leicester.

References

Armstrong, M. (1980). *Closely Observed Children: Diary of a Primary Classroom*. London, Writers & Readers.

Aspin, D. (1986). 'Objectivity and assessment in the arts: the problem of aesthetic education', in M. Ross (ed.), *Assessment in Arts Education*. Oxford, Pergamon Press.

Bennett, N. (1987). 'The search for the effective primary school teacher', in S. Delamont (ed.), *The Primary School Teacher*. London, Falmer Press.

Bennett, N., Desforges, C., Cockburn, A. and Wilkinson, B. (1984). *The Quality of Pupil Learning Experiences*. London, Lawrence Erlbaum.

Boden, M. A. (1979). *Piaget*. London, Fontana.

Brophy, J. E. and Good, T. L. (1986). 'Teacher behaviour and student achievement', in M. C. Wittrock (ed.), *Handbook of Research on Teaching*, 3rd edn. New York, Macmillan.

Brown, G. and Desforges, C. (1979). *Piaget's Theory: A Psychological Critique*. London, Routledge & Kegan Paul.

Bruner, J. S. and Haste, H. (1987). *Making Sense: The Child's Construction of the World*. London, Methuen.

Bruner, J. S., Olver, R. R. and Greenfield, P. M. (eds.) (1966). *Studies in Cognitive Growth*. New York, John Wiley.

Calouste Gulbenkian Foundation (1982). *The Arts in Schools: Principles, Practice and Provision*. London, Calouste Gulbenkian Foundation.

Delamont, S. and Galton, M. (1987). 'The ORACLE and the muses: aesthetic activity in six schools', in L. Tickle (ed.), *The Arts in Education: Some Research Studies*. Beckenham, Kent, Croom Helm.

DES (1983). *Aesthetic Development*. London, Assessment of Performance Unit.

(1987a). *The National Curriculum 5–16: A Consultation Document*. London, DES and the Welsh Office.

(1987b). *National Curriculum Task Group on Assessment and Testing: A Report*. London, DES and the Welsh Office.

Doyle, W. (1979). 'Classroom tasks and student abilities', in P. Peterson and H. Walberg (eds.), *Research on Teaching: Concepts, Findings and Implications*. Berkeley, Calif., McCutchan.

(1986). 'Classroom organisation and management', in M. C. Wittrock (ed.), *Handbook of Research on Teaching*, 3rd edn. New York, Macmillan.

Eisner, E. W. (1976). 'What we know about children's art – and what we need to know', in E. W. Eisner (ed.), *The Arts, Human Development, and Education*. Berkeley, Calif., McCutchan.

Gage, N. L. and Berliner, D. C. (1984). *Educational Psychology*. 3rd edn. Boston, Houghton Mifflin.

Galton, M. (1987). 'An ORACLE chronicle: a decade of classroom research'. *Teaching and Teacher Education*, 3: 299–313.
Gardner, H. (1973). *The Arts and Human Development*. New York, John Wiley.
   (1976). 'Unfolding or teaching: on the optimal training of artistic skills', in E. W. Eisner (ed.), *The Arts, Human Development, and Education*. Berkeley, Calif., McCutchan.
   (1983). *Frames of Mind: The Theory of Multiple Intelligences*. London, Paladin.
Gardner, H. and Grunbaum, J. (1986). 'The assessment of artistic thinking: comments on the national assessment of educational progress in the arts'. Unpublished paper, Harvard Project Zero.
Hargreaves, D. H. (1983). 'The teaching of art and the art of teaching: towards an alternative view of aesthetic learning'. in M. Hammersley and A. Hargreaves (eds.), *Curriculum Practice: Some Sociological Case Studies*. London, Falmer.
Lovell, K. (1958). *Educational Psychology and Children*. London, University of London Press.
Madsen, C. K. and Yarborough, C. (1980). *Competency-based Music Education*. Englewood Cliffs, NJ, Prentice-Hall.
Modgil, S., Modgil, C. and Brown, G. (eds.) (1983). *Jean Piaget: An Interdisciplinary Critique*. London, Routledge & Kegan Paul.
Plowden Report (1967). *Children and Their Primary Schools: A Report of the Central Advisory Council for Education*. London, HMSO.
Ross, M. (ed.) (1982). *The Development of Aesthetic Experience*. Oxford, Pergamon Press.
   (ed.) (1986). *Assessment in Arts Education*. Oxford, Pergamon Press.
Rowlands, S. (1984). *The Enquiring Classroom*. London, Falmer Press.
Sloboda, J. A. (1985). *The Musical Mind: The Cognitive Psychology of Music*. Oxford, Oxford University Press.
Swanwick, K. (1988). 'The relevance of research: too little theory', in A. E. Kemp (ed.), *Research in Music Education: A Festschrift for Arnold Bentley*. London, International Society for Music Education.
Tickle, L. (ed.) (1987). *The Arts in Education: Some Research Studies*. Beckenham, Kent, Croom Helm.
Tizard, B. and Hughes, M. (1984). *Young Children Learning: Talking and Thinking at Home and at School*. London, Fontana.
Vygotsky, L. S. (1978). *Mind in Society: The Development of Higher Psychological Processes*. Cambridge, Mass., Harvard University Press.
Wallas, G. (1926). *The Art of Thought*. London, Watts.
Wexler-Sherman, C., Gardner, H. and Feldman, D. H. (1988). 'A pluralistic view of early assessment: the Project Spectrum approach'. *Theory into Practice*, 27: 77–83.
Wolf, D. P. (1988a). 'Artistic learning: what and where is it?' *Journal of Aesthetic Education*, 22: 143–55.
   (1988b). 'Opening up assessment: ideas from the arts'. *Educational Leadership*, 45: 24–9.
Wood, D. J. (1987). 'Aspects of teaching and learning', in M. P. M. Richards and P. H. Light (eds.), *Children of Social Worlds*. Oxford, Basil Blackwell.
   (1988). *How Children Think and Learn*. Oxford, Basil Blackwell.
Wood, D. J., Bruner, J. S. and Ross, G. (1976). 'The role of tutoring in problem solving'. *Journal of Child Psychology and Psychiatry*, 17: 89–100.
Wood, D. J. and Middleton, D. J. (1975). 'A study of assisted problem solving'. *British Journal of Psychology*, 66: 181–91.

Author index

Subject index